Buddhism

Buddhism

Thomas Berry

ANIMA

Cover photo. Eyes of the Buddha looking from the Swayambhu Stupa over the Kathmandu Valley to find and aid those in need.

Anima Edition, 1989

Manufactured in the United States of America

Anima Publications
1053 Wilson Avenue
Chambersburg, PA 17201

ISBN 0-89012-01

CONTENTS

ABBREVIATIONS

An.—*Anguttara Nikaya*
D.—*Digha Nikaya*
Dh.—*Dhammapada*
HOS—Harvard Oriental Series
Iti.—*Itivuttakam*
Katha.—*Kathavatthu*
Maj.—*Majjhima Nikaya*
Mil.—*Milindapanho*
PTS—Pali Text Society
Samy.—*Samyutta Nikaya*
SBB—Sacred Books of the Buddhists
SBE—Sacred Books of the East
Sn.—*Sutta Nipata*
Vim.—*Vimalikirtinirdesa*
Vis.—*Visuddhimagga*

Full bibliographical details are given in the Bibliography.
References to Pali scriptures are generally to the page in
the Pali text indicated within parentheses in the English
translations which are generally from the publications of the
Pali Text Society, the Sacred Books of the Buddhists, or
from the Sacred Books of the East. References to the
Dhammapada and Sutta Nipata are by verse number. References to Mahayana texts such as the *Lotus Sutra* are by
chapter and verse.

PART I

EARLY BUDDHISM

CHAPTER I

LIFE OF SIDDHARTHA GOTAMA

Siddhartha Gotama was born in Kapilavastu, in the foothills of the Himalaya Mountains, in the year 566 B.C. The Gotama were a division of the Sakya, a warrior kingdom in the northeastern region of India. Later, after his spiritual enlightenment in 531, Siddhartha became known as Buddha, the Enlightened One. He was also called Sakyamuni, the Sage of the Sakya.

He came, apparently, from a family of some status. The only records that mention his early life describe it as one of comfort, even of luxury, although in truth he lived in a rather primitive setting. In any case, this was not a satisfying existence to Siddhartha. During his early years, he thought deeply over the human condition, the turmoil, the disappointments and frustrations to which man is subject. He was most affected by his growing awareness of the withering effects of age on the human body. There were also disease and finally death to be faced by all men. The inevitability of these afflictions led Siddhartha to long-sustained reflection on the very nature of human life itself. Seeing others suffering from the debilitating effects of age, he thought, "Now I too am subject to old age and decay, not having passed beyond old age and decay. Thus considering the matter, all pride in my youth deserted me" (*An.* i, 145). These afflictions did not affect merely the body of man, nor were they incidental to the life of man. They were afflictions of the mind and the entire being of man. They were so constant as to be identical with the life process itself.

Buddha was not the only person in India at this time to feel the sorrow of life so intensely and to concern himself with a remedy. Many wandering holy men of India were searching for a spiritual discipline that would enable man not only to deal with sorrow successfully but to root it out totally and permanently from human life itself. These men, mendicant recluses, wandered back and forth across north India in their unending quest for a higher life experience that would bring to human existence the transformation that was needed. They had gone forth from their homes into the homeless life so that this spiritual quest would be their only occupation. Abandoning all possessions they lived on the meagre alms given by the people. Buddha himself was inspired by these men. At the age of twenty-nine, he too went forth from his home to become a recluse.

He first put himself under the spiritual guidance of the recluses Alara Kalama and Uddakha Rajaputta. Following their meditative discipline, he sought a solution for life's sorrow as an inner illumination. Yet Buddha soon found that these guides had themselves not attained the insight needed for a proper understanding of the human condition and for a truly liberating experience; they could not guide anyone else to what they themselves did not know.

Separating himself from these two spiritual masters, he continued as a wandering recluse for some six years. Part of this time he spent with five companions. Together they undertook an austere discipline in quest of a true healing for the sorrow of life. The austerities they practiced involved an intense effort on the part of Buddha, an effort that culminated in the severity of a great fast. In the account given later of this fast, he said:

> Just like a row of reed-knots my backbone stood out through lack of sustenance. Just as the rafters of a tottering house fall

in this way and that, so did my ribs fall in this way and that through lack of sustenance. Just as in a deep, deep well the sparkle of the waters may be seen sunk in the deeps below, so in the depths of their sockets did the lustre of my eyes seem sunk, through lack of sustenance. Just as a bitter gourd, cut off unripened from the stalk, is shrivelled and withered by wind and sun, so was the very skin of my head shrivelled and withered through lack of food (*Maj.* i, 242–248).

Yet after all this he failed to attain the goal he was seeking. Austerity was not the answer.

At this time he became aware of the need both for a new type of effort and for a new depth of understanding. The problem was more one of mental concentration than of physical austerity. Austerity only weakened man in his physical faculties and left him without the energy needed for intensive mental application. He spent one night at Gaya in meditation so intense that it brought him to the ecstatic experience he was seeking. This moment in the life of Buddha is one of the most significant moments in the spiritual history of mankind. The illumination that broke over his mind has ever since flowed over the greater part of Asia in a great tide of spiritual healing. For centuries the peoples of Asia have walked in the radiance of this light. It has influenced their lives more extensively and more profoundly than any other spiritual tradition.

The enlightenment itself consisted of a profound awareness that all things of earth are impermanent, sorrowful, insubstantial. What is born begins to die as soon as it is born. This is the ultimate cause of all sorrow. Man becomes attached to things mentally and emotionally as though they were substantial, abiding realities. Then he is thrown into a state of anguish as the objects of his attachment disintegrate. In a special manner, man experiences this pain within his own being. Change is itself anguish. There is no escape from this experience so long as man remains within the unending cycle of time and its transformations.

Because a special type of ignorance is at the root of this primordial sorrow of man, true understanding would reveal to him the insubstantial nature of the world. This in turn would lead to the cessation of attachment. Cessation of attachment, sufficiently profound, would lift man to an experience in which he would escape all affliction in the relief of Nirvana. He would have passed from the conditioned world to the world of the unconditioned. But nothing was possible so long as men refused to face life with this devastating directness. A type of moral courage was needed which few men possess. Thus their self-imposed ignorance, a fatal obstacle to salvation. "Monks, I do not see any other single obstacle which has so hindered mankind and caused man for so long a time to fare up and down and endlessly wander on like this obstacle of ignorance" (*Iti.* 8).

After his own illumination, Buddha remained several weeks at Gaya in ecstatic joy over his enlightenment. There was, however, a further crisis through which he had to pass. A hard decision had to be made concerning his mission to mankind. He was tempted to go his way as a solitary recluse. "If I were to teach this illumination and others did not understand me, that would be a weariness that would be a vexation to me" (*Maj.* i, 168). In explaining this attitude of Buddha's a later work tells us:

> That his heart inclined not to the preaching of the truth, but to inaction, was because he saw, on the one hand, how profound and abstruse was the Doctrine, how hard to grasp and understand, how subtle, how difficult to penetrate into; and, on the other, how devoted beings are to the satisfaction of their lusts, how firmly possessed by false notions of individualism. And so he wavered at the thought, Whom shall I teach? (*Mil.* 233).

Yet it was unendurable for him to hear the complaint: "Alas, the world is lost, alas, the world is destroyed, for the mind of the Tathagata, the perfect one, the fully awakened

one, inclines to little effort and not to teaching the saving
Truth" (*Maj.* i, 168). On his final decision to undertake a
mission to mankind he proclaimed: "Opened for those who
hear are the doors of the Deathless, Brahma, let them give
forth their faith" (*Maj.* i, 169). Later it would be said: "A
being not liable to delusion has arisen in the world for the
welfare of the manyfolk, for the happiness of the manyfolk,
out of compassion for the world, for the good, the welfare,
the happiness of gods and men" (*Maj.* i, 83).

After making his decision, Buddha went to seek out the
five recluses, his former companions. After years of spiritual effort, they would understand and accept the spiritual
vision he would now offer to the world. He found them at
Benares, the holy city of India. There in Deer Park, just outside the city, he proclaimed for the first time the Four Noble
Truths and the Noble Eightfold Path which ever since have
constituted the Buddhist Way of Perfection.

The Fourfold Truth states that sorrow is universal in this
world of change; that desire is the cause of sorrow; that extinction of sorrow comes about by the extinction of desire;
that the way to extinguish desire is through the eightfold
path of right view, right intention, right speech, right action,
right livelihood, right effort, right mindfulness, right concentration. Thus is constituted the Middle Path of Buddhist
teaching.

At the end of his discourse, the five recluses became the
first followers of Buddha. Thus began a public ministry that
lasted for the next forty-five years. During this period Buddha went to all the major cities in the eastern region of the
Ganges basin: Westward as far as Mathura, eastward as far
as Rajagriha and Campi, north as far as Lumbini and Kapilavastu, south as far as Gaya. These cities in general delin-
eate the area in which Buddha travelled and preached, an
area that included all the seven major kingdoms of the region: Kasi, Kosala, Anga, Magadha, Kuru, Vajji, and Malla.

Buddha established a close friendship with several of the

rulers of the period. He was especially close to King Bimbisara of Magadha and to Posanandi, king of Kosala. Bimbisara, in particular, can be considered as a forerunner of Asoka in his concern for the Buddhist monks and for the message they carried to the people. Posanandi, who met Buddha shortly after Buddha began his preaching, frequently visited him and discussed the way of salvation.

The wealthy people of this region also responded vigorously to the teaching of Buddha. They assisted by furnishing the monks with the things they needed. Also the Brahmanical ascetics, the Jatilas, came to listen. Many were converted. He held discussions with the other ascetics of the region, especially with the Jains and Ajivakas. Both of these had strong views on the way of perfection. In the judgment of Buddha, the Jains were too ascetic, the Ajivakas too fatalistic. Buddha often spoke with the Brahman priests. Many of his early followers came from this highest caste of Brahmanism.

Yet everyone was welcome, from whatever social strata. Buddha did not oppose or seek to change the structure of Indian society at the time. He insisted only that there was a spiritual aspect of life available to all mankind, that social standing had nothing to do with inner spiritual perfection. This spiritual perfection, the only true nobility, was available to all. Thus, he spoke of the True Brahman as one who was leading a spiritually elevated life, one completely detached from desire for things of this phenomenal world. Salvation was not obtained by ritual, by superstition, or by some heavenly grace. Salvation was the result of an inner spiritual transformation whereby men pass from the cyclic world of time and change to an experience of the timeless and immortal.

As the end of his life approached, Buddha, with Ananda, the constant companion of his later years, journeyed for the last time through north India to the city of Kusinagara, above the Ganges in the foothills of the Himalayas. There, after a series of parting instructions to Ananda, he died, in

486 B.C. His body was cremated according to the custom of the period. Afterwards, stupas were erected to house the relics that survived the cremation. The stupa, from earlier centuries in India, was a memorial for a king who had died. Thus, in the stories that come down to us, Buddha, after his death, was given royal honours.

This, in simple form, is the story of Buddha's life. Considering the large numbers of such mendicants in India at the time, it would seem merely the account of someone belonging to the same class of men as the others, with perhaps a little more insight into the basic issues of man's spiritual formation and the manner in which to deal with the human condition.

Yet this simple account of Buddha's life contains, in itself, the story of the person who more than anyone else has dominated the life and culture of Asian peoples. He carried within himself one of earth's deepest mysteries, a mystery so profound that it is sometimes said that an understanding of Buddha and the teaching he gave to mankind will be one of the last and highest attainments of the human mind.

CHAPTER II

SORROW

Buddha's life and teaching were dominated by his experience of the sorrow inherent in the human condition. All his efforts were devoted to discovering a way of dealing with this sorrow. He remained confident throughout his life that the human condition could be transcended, if only men would undertake the intensive spiritual effort required. The liberating vision once attained would enable a person to disengage himself completely from all illusion and from attachments to the visible world. The bliss attained in this liberating experience he described as the extinction of all forms of existence that we know in this life. But it is clear from the entire body of his teaching that this extinction of all earthly consciousness was only the introduction to some experience that is totally other than what we experience here.

The problem of sorrow is to be solved, not by altering the external conditions of life, but by strengthening man inwardly, enabling him to rise above the world of change to an inner experience that would permanently remove him from subjection to the agonizing experience of temporal existence. Of Buddha's early life we are told:

> Thus, O monks, before my enlightenment, while yet a Bodhisattva and not fully enlightened, being myself subject to birth, I sought out the nature of birth; being subject to old age I sought out the nature of old age, of sickness, of death, of sorrow, of impurity. Then I thought, What if I being myself subject to birth were to seek out the nature of

birth . . . and having seen the wretchedness of the nature of birth, were to seek out the unborn, the supreme peace of Nirvana (*Maj.* i, 163).

This led Buddha to enter into the homeless life. "Now at that time, while yet a boy, black-haired, in the prime of youth, in the first stage of life, while my unwilling mother and father wept with tear-stained faces, I cut off my hair and beard, and putting on yellow robes went forth from home to a homeless life" (*Maj.* i, 240).

His later teaching was increasingly centred on this problem of sorrow. The general and most consistent answer he gave to questions concerning his teaching was: "I have expounded what pain is; I have expounded the origin of pain; I have expounded the cessation of pain; I have expounded the method by which men may attain the cessation of pain" (*D.* i, 189). He gave a powerful summary of his teaching in the expression: "Brethren, the mighty ocean has but one flavour, the flavour of salt, even so brethren, has my teaching but one flavour, the flavour of release" (*Udana* 56).

An all-pervading delusion was at the root of this anguish experienced by mankind so constantly and so universally. "They who, giving up delusion, have pierced right through the mass of gloom, wander on no longer: There is in them no longer any cause for that" (*Iti.* 8).

This release from ignorance required a direct confrontation with reality in its most stark expression. The capacity to face reality with total fearlessness was seldom found among men. That was the basic reason why men, attached to things of this visible world, became so deeply involved in the disintegrating processes of time. The answer was to develop in men a capacity to face reality with unflinching directness. Of Buddha himself it was said: "By comprehending all the world in all the world just as it is, from all the world is he released, in all the world he clings to naught" (*An.* ii, 25). All of this is reduced to a twofold proposition: "To look at evil as evil is the first instruction. After seeing evil as evil, be disgusted with it, be cleansed from it, be liberated from it: this is the second instruction" (*Iti.* 33).

When men look fearlessly at the world, they discover: "Everything is impermanent, every being in its parts and in its functions. Growth is the nature of things, growth and decay. Things are produced, they dissolve: That is best when finally they have passed away" (*D.* 198, 199).

An even deeper insight into things, when examined with truly piercing insight, is that there is no abiding reality beneath the phenomenal world. All things, in the very depth of their being, are in a state of flux. Even in living things, there is no abiding soul. The cyclic process of unending change does not affect merely the surface part of a being. Change affects every being in its most elemental structure. Change is total. As the flame of a candle is not the same from one moment to the next, so no being is the same from one moment to the next. Nothing substantial passes over from one momentary existence to the other. Each momentary existence is itself real enough. Yet it has the reality of something that comes into being and disappears as a single process. Each moment of existence conditions the next moment of existence; but there is no abiding subject that binds all these moments together. There is no substance, no soul, no personality.

This insubstantial aspect of things extends beyond the physical world to the mind and to its states of consciousness:

> Thus do I, Aggivessane, train disciples, and by such divisions does the great part of my instruction for disciples proceed: Material shape, monks, is impermanent, feeling is impermanent, perception is impermanent, the habitual tendencies are impermanent, consciousness is impermanent. Material shape, monks, is not self, feeling is not self, perception is not self, the habitual tendencies are not self, consciousness is not self; all conditioned things are impermanent, all things are not self (*Maj.* i, 230).

Every consciousness whatever, be it past, future, or present, be it inward or outward, gross or subtle, low or high, far or near—every consciousness, I say, must be thus regarded as it really is by right insight: "This is not mine; this am not I; this is not the self of me" (*Samy.* iii, 68).

The original deception at the root of man's attachment to the phenomenal world is man's conviction that he exists. The highest spiritual advice that can be given anyone is: "Let him by insight destroy, as the root cause of man's difficulty, all such thought as 'I am'" (*Sn.* 916). This leads to the highest metaphysical teaching of Buddhism, the teaching concerning emptiness, or *sunyata*. The final wisdom is that which,

Knows of the world, "All is unreal."
Knows without greed, "All is unreal."
Knows without passion, "All is unreal."
Knows without hate, "All is unreal."
Knows undeceived, "All is unreal" (*Sn.* 9–13).

One of the final meditations in the Buddhist ascent to spiritual liberation is meditation on the proposition: "There is not anything" (*Maj.* iii, 38). This enables a person to pass beyond the plane of neither perception nor nonperception. When finally there is a complete stopping of perception and feeling, then final release is attained, the highest spiritual attainment in the Buddhist path of perfection is reached. A person has passed beyond the sorrow of life (*Maj.* iii, 28).

It is not surprising to learn that Buddha constantly repeated what he once said to Vaccha, who questioned him concerning his teaching. "Vaccha, this teaching is deep, difficult to see, difficult to understand, peaceful, excellent, beyond dialectic, subtle, intelligible to the wise; but it is hard for you who are of another view, another allegiance, another objective, or a different observance, and under a distant master" (*Maj.* i, 487). On another occasion Buddha is reported as saying, "The wisdom I teach is difficult to understand, difficult to practise" (*Sn.* 701).

So difficult is this teaching that until the time of Buddha no one had so truly or so fully realized this hard truth concerning the impermanent, insubstantial nature of the phenomenal world. Nor had anyone provided a way of managing the human condition and attaining the release that all men desire. "About this a Tathagata is fully enlightened, he fully understands it. So enlightened and understanding he declares, teaches and makes it plain. He shows it forth, he opens it up, explains and makes it clear: This fact that all phenomena are impermanent" (*An.* i, 286).

Yet once attained a startling process is initiated. There comes about a complete reversal of values. A spiritual experience of extraordinary significance takes place. All the tensions of life are suddenly released. There comes about a salvation experience of exceptional dimensions.

CHAPTER III

THE SALVATION EXPERIENCE

The Buddhist experience of the nothingness of things, shattering in its impact, must be considered a mental purification absolutely necessary for the joy that follows. This joy breaks forth so suddenly and with such exuberance that it startles the reader who first encounters the more brilliant expressions of this experience. There is, above all, a sublime feeling of release from all the bonds that fetter man within his temporal habitation. "Now thou art seen, thou builder of the house, never again shalt thou build me a house. All my rafters are broken, shattered the roof-beam; my thoughts are purified of illusion; the extinction of craving has been won" (*Dh.* 154). These words, the classical expression of the Buddhist salvation experience, are considered to be those spoken by Buddha himself at the moment of his enlightenment.

The explosive quality of this new experience is felt in the *Sutra Nipata:* "He who bursts every bond within, destroys its root without, and frees himself from the very source of every bond and restraint, he is the noble one" (*Sn.* 532).

Yet this final joy is an experience that completes an earlier joy attained in the meditation discipline of Buddhism. When the person meditating enters the second stage of meditation,

He drenches, saturates, permeates, suffuses this very body with the rapture and joy that are born of concentration; there is no part of his whole body that is not suffused with the rapture and joy that are born of concentration. Udayin, as a pool of water with water welling up within it, but which has no inlet for water from the eastern . . . western . . . northern . . . or from the southern side, and even if the god did not send down showers upon it from time to time, yet a current of water having welled up in that pool would drench, saturate, permeate, suffuse that pool with cool water; there would be no part of that pool that was not suffused with cool water—even so, Udayin, does a monk drench, saturate. . . . there is no part of his whole body that is not suffused with the rapture and joy that are born of concentration (*Maj.* ii, 15, 16).

Yet this experience is not confined to the person himself. In this stage of meditation the joy, friendliness, serenity, equanimity are, in moments of profound reflection, immediately radiated over the entire world: "A monk abides having suffused the whole world everywhere, in every way, with a mind of equanimity that is far-reaching, widespread, immeasurable, without enmity, without malevolence. This, your reverence, is called immeasurable freedom of mind" (*Maj.* i, 297).

The final stage when the mind emerges into the totally unstructured world of the transphenomenal is foreshadowed in the emergence of the person from his physical body into a mind-formed body. This release is pictured as a drawing forth from the conditioned forms of existence.

Again, Udayin, a course has been pointed out by me for disciples, practising which disciples of mine from this body [mentally] produce [another] body, having material shape, mind-made, having all its major and minor parts, not deficient in any sense-organ. As, Udayin, a man might draw an arrow from a reed and might think thus: "This is the reed, this the arrow, the reed is one thing, the arrow another; it is from the reed that the arrow has been drawn"; or again, Udayin, as a man might draw a sword from the scabbard and might think thus: "This is the sword, this the scabbard, the sword is one thing, the scabbard another; it is from the scabbard that the sword has been drawn"; or again, Udayin, as a man might take a snake out of the slough and might think thus: "This is the snake, this the slough, the snake is one thing, the slough another: It is from the slough that the snake has been taken" —even so, Udayin, a course has been pointed out by me for disciples, practising which my disciples from this body produce a body . . . not deficient in any sense-organ. As to this, many of my disciples abide having attained to this accomplishment and to going beyond through super-knowledge (*Maj.* ii, 16).

This emergence from a lower to a higher order, this drawing forth of a hidden splendour, this breaking forth from confinement to liberation, this being clothed with a new life, are all expressions that Buddhism has in common with many other spiritual traditions of man, especially those with mystical tendencies. In Buddhist writings these descriptions are especially vivid.

One of the loveliest comparisons is that of a tiny chick breaking through its shell. Just as a mother hen might think,

"O may my chicks, having pierced through the egg-shells with the point of the claw on their feet or with their beaks, break forth safely," for these chicks were ones who were able to break forth safely having pierced through the egg-shells with the point of the claw on their feet or with their beaks. Even so, monks, is it that a monk who is thus possessed of the fifteen factors including exertion becomes one . . . for winning the incomparable security from the bonds (*Maj.* i, 104).

Kaccana, it is like a young baby boy lying on his back and bound around his neck with a fivefold swaddling, it might be with swaddlings of thread. As he grows up and develops his faculties, he would be released from those swaddlings, and in the absence of swaddlings he would know: "I am released." Even so, Kaccana, let there come intelligent men, guileless,

honest, straight. . . . Even so, indeed, is deliverance from
the direct bond, that is from the bond of ignorance (*Maj.*
ii, 44).

A person having this salvation experience is in the same
situation as Buddha, also known as the Tathagata. He is
beyond all ordinary designation: "The Tathagata can no
longer be designated as being matter, sensations, ideas, voli-
tions, knowledge: he is freed from these designations; he is
deep, immeasurable, unfathomable, like the great ocean.
One cannot say: he is, he is not, he is and he is not. He
neither is nor is not" (*Samy.* iv, 374). Such a person has
passed beyond the *dvandva,* the dualities in which ordinary
human thought is expressed.

Passage from the visible world is complete: "Where water,
earth, fire, air find no footing, there shine no stars, nor is the
sun displayed there. There gleams no moon; no darkness
there is seen. So when the sage, the Brahman, by wisdom of
his own self has pierced to the truth, he is freed from form
and no-form, from pleasure and pain" (*Udana* 9).

The proper name for this final release in Buddhist tradition is *Nirvana,* a word that indicates a total liberation from
the human condition. When questioned concerning the explanation of Nirvana, Nagasena replied: "Nirvana, O King,
has nothing similar to it. By no metaphor, or explanation, or
reasoning, or argument can its form or figure, or duration, or
measure be made clear" (*Mil.* 316).

But while its form cannot be made clear to man, something
of its qualities can be indicated.

As ghee is beautiful in color, O King, so also is Nirvana
beautiful in righteousness. And again, O King, as ghee has
a pleasant perfume, so also has Nirvana the pleasant perfume
of righteousness. This is the second quality of ghee inherent
in Nirvana. And again, O King, as ghee has a pleasant taste, so
also has Nirvana. This is the third quality of ghee inherent in
Nirvana (*Mil.* 322).

When asked as regards the place where Nirvana is stored up, the answer is:

> There is no spot, O King, where Nirvana is situated, and yet Nirvana is, and he who orders his life right will, by careful attention, realize Nirvana. Just as fire exists, and yet there is no place where fire is so stored up (*Mil.* 327).

But is there no place on which a person can stand and realize Nirvana?

> Virtue, O King, is the place. For if grounded in virtue, and careful in attention—whether in the land of the Scythians or the Greeks, whether in China or Tartary, whether in Alexandria or in Nikumba, whether in Benares or in Kosala, wherever he may be, the man who orders his life aright will realize Nirvana (*Mil.* 327).

A deeper reflection on the nature of Nirvana is also given by Nagasena in his classical conversation with the Greek king, Menander.

> Nirvana, O King, is unproducible, and no cause for its origin has been declared. . . . And why? Because Nirvana is not put together of any qualities. . . . It is uncompounded, not made of anything. Of Nirvana, O King, it cannot be said that it has been produced, or not been produced, or that it can be produced, that it is past or future or present, that it is perceptible by the eye or the ear or the nose or the tongue or by the sense of touch.
>
> "But if so, Nagasena, then you are only showing us how Nirvana is a condition that does not exist. There can be no such thing as Nirvana."
>
> Nirvana exists, O King. And it is perceptible to the mind. By means of his pure heart, refined and straight, free from the obstacles, free from low cravings, that disciple of the Noble Ones who has fully attained can see Nirvana (*Mil.* 268).

The person who has reached the higher levels of Buddhist meditation passes beyond the realm of perception and nonperception. When he finally enters and abides in the stopping of perception and feeling, then he "does not imagine he is aught or anywhere or in anything" (*Maj.* iii, 45). This is one of the more precise descriptions of Nirvana.

The Buddhist way of perfection was not for the purpose of any gain, either moral or intellectual. Nirvana is its own purpose, its own sufficient explanation. "So it is, monks, that this noble faring is not for advantage in gains, honours, fame; it is not for advantage in moral habit; it is not for advantage in concentration, it is not for advantage in knowledge and vision. That, monks, which is unshakable freedom of mind, this is the goal, monks, of this noble-faring, this the pith, this the culmination" (*Maj.* i, 197). Because Nirvana is not rightly called morally good, "We cannot predicate of its disinterestedness, love, intelligence, faith, energy, mindfulness, concentration, understanding. Nirvana is beyond such predications" (*Katha.* xix, 6).

Among the most impressive descriptions of Nirvana is that given in the *Udana:* "There is, brethren, an unborn, a not-become, a not-made, a not-compounded. If, brethren, ther were no unborn, not-become, not-made, not-compounded, there could be no escape from what is born, become, made, and compounded" (*Udana* 80). Another definition of Nirvana is the simple statement: "The cessation of becoming is Nirvana" (*Samy.* ii, 68).

It is important to understand that this experience of Nirvana is not delayed until after death. "Monk, if he is freed by this turning away, by dispassion in regard to these things, by their cessation, it is fitting to call him a monk who has attained Nirvana here and now" (*Samy.* iii, 163, 164).

While those who experience Nirvana themselves have a direct knowledge of Nirvana, those with no direct experience can also know something of it. "Just so, O King, it is by hearing the glad words of those who have seen Nirvana, that

they who have not perceived it know how happy a state it
is" (*Mil.* 69).

Release from all the bonds of this world brings a sublime
and lasting serenity.

If only one could reach a state in which there were no becoming, there would be calm, that would be sweet—the cessation of all these conditions, the getting rid of all these defects, the end of cravings, the absence of passion, peace,
Nirvana! And forthwith does his mind leap forward into
that state in which there is no becoming, and then he has
found peace, then he exults and rejoices at the thought: "A
refuge have I found at last!" And he strives with might and
main along that path, searches it out, accustoms himself
thoroughly to it, to that end he makes firm his self-posses-
sion, to that end he holds fast in effort, to that end he remains steadfast in love and to that he directs his mind again
and again, until gone far beyond the transitory, he gains the
Real, the highest fruit. When he has gained that, O King,
that man who has ordered his life aright has realized [seen
face to face] Nirvana (*Mil.* 326).

CHAPTER IV

BUDDHA

This delight in salvation flowed back over the person who brought this salvation, over the doctrine that enlightened mankind concerning this salvation, over the community of those sharing this salvation and communicating it to others. Thus the high praise met with in Buddhism for Buddha, Dharma, Sangha—Buddha, his Teaching, the Community. These three, called the Three Jewels of Buddhism, constitute the Threefold Refuge to which those who accept Buddhism go for relief from sorrow. The famous formula of the Buddhist vows is: I go for refuge to the Buddha. I go for refuge to Dharma. I go for refuge to the Sangha.

Endless praise of the Three Jewels rings in Buddhist scriptures:

Praise, you who dwell on earth or in the heavens,
Let every being praise the Buddha, thus come, dear to gods
    and men;
Let joy prevail!

Praise, you who dwell on earth or in the heavens,
Let every being praise the Doctrine, now arrived, dear to
    gods and men;
Let joy prevail!

Praise you who dwell on earth or in the heavens,
Let every being praise the Order, now arrived, dear to gods
    and men;
Let joy prevail! (*Sn.* 236–238).

Of these three, the first, Buddha himself, is by far the most significant and the one most exalted in Buddhist tradition. The other two might be considered as various forms in which the Buddha reality appears. The term "Buddha" indicates a type of being who appears in different aeons of time for the salvation of mankind. Each Buddha has a universal mission to mankind in a certain aeon of time. Two Buddhas could not appear in the same world, for the world itself would explode under the impact of two such vast experiences.

Siddhartha Gotama, Sakyamuni, the Buddha of this historical age, constitutes the central reality of this aeon of time. He is not simply an exceptional human person. He is the omniscient one, the supreme teacher, the bearer of all life's meaning, the guide to release from suffering—the only such guide.

In the centuries since Buddha's own time, the salvation experience he provided has flowed over India and most of Asia eastward from Persia. Nothing before or since has given this part of Asia such realism in its confrontation with the sorrow of life, or such hope for a blissful release from this sorrow. The response has been joy in the doctrine, praise of its author. The reader can see from the earliest documents how the surging devotion to Buddha rose visibly from century to century. Originally a human teacher, a guide, as many other spiritual guides to the people of those centuries, Buddha surpassed them all in the realism of his teaching and in the sublimity of his vision. His guidance evoked a response totally unlike that of any other spiritual leader of Asia.

Looked upon as a saviour-personality, he became progressively identified with that transcendent experience of which he spoke so often. Thus Buddha in his own person became the centre of unlimited affection. He was considered "the bestower of immortality" (*An.* v, 226, 256). He appeared on the world scene as the dawn of a new radiance: "In pity you revealed the saving Truth and unveiled all, pure seer, to flood the world with light" (*Sn.* 378). Buddha is spoken of as noblest of all mankind, peerless in all the worlds, as the fully illumined one, the Teacher, the Sage (*Sn.* 544, 538).

Most often in the canonical writings, Buddha is addressed: "Perfect, fully awakened, is the exalted One, abounding in wisdom and goodness, happy, with knowledge of the worlds, unsurpassed as a guide to mortals willing to be led, the teacher of gods and men, a blessed Buddha" (*D.* i, 49). Another passage, repeated many times in Buddhist scriptures, describes the work of Buddha in these terms:

> Just as if a man were to set up that which is thrown down, or were to reveal that which is hidden away, or were to point out the right road to him who has gone astray, or were to bring a lamp into the darkness, so that those who have eyes can see external forms—just so, Lord, has the truth been made known to me, in many a figure, by the Blessed One (*D.* ii, 132).

So identified is Buddha with the final reality of things that he is spoken of as the one "whose name is Truth" (*An.* iv, 283). He was not ordained as were the other members of the Order. His illumination at Gaya was itself his ordination (*Mil.* 76). Having seen what no one else had seen, he had become the "lifter of the veil" (*Sn.* 372), that all might see and understand the true nature of things in this world and attain the saving vision that leads to Nirvana.

All of these designations are implied in a unique term of the highest significance given to Buddha, the term *Tathagata*. Few terms in the entire range of Buddhist terminology are so difficult to comprehend as this one. It must have existed prior to the time of Buddha to designate a prophetic personality with a salvation mission to all mankind. Many descriptions are given of Buddha under this title:

> The Tathagata, brethren, is a perfect One, is fully enlightened. He it is who causes a way to arise which had not arisen before; who brings about a way not brought about before; who proclaims a way not proclaimed before; who is

the knower of a way, who understands a way, who is skilled in a way. And now, brethren, his disciples are wayfarers who follow after him. That, brethren, is the distinction, the specific feature which distinguishes the Tathagata, who, being a perfect One, is fully enlightened, from those of the brethren who are freed by insight (*Samy.* iii, 66).

One of the distinctive accomplishments of the Tathagata is that

> He, by himself, thoroughly understands and sees, as it were, face to face this universe—the world below with all its spirits, the worlds above, of Mara and Brahma—and all creatures, Samanas and Brahmans, gods and men, and he then makes his knowledge known to others. The truth he proclaims both in its letter and in its spirit, lovely in its origin, lovely in its progress, lovely in its consummation; the higher life he makes known in all its purrity, in all its perfection (*D.* i, 46).

Also in his own being, his own way, in his unique spiritual conquest he has attained what cannot be attained by any other. "His conquest cannot be accomplished again; into his conquest no one enters; by what track then can you lead him, the Awakened, the one of unlimited insight, the trackless one. By what track can you lead him, whom no desire with its seductions and its poisons can lead astray, the Awakened, the one of unlimited insight, the trackless" (*Dh.* 179, 180).

Such a person could not be considered as just another one of many great personalities known and praised extensively in one of the traditional societies of mankind. Seen by his followers as a unique saviour-type personality, he was a bringer of salvation, the supreme good sought by man. He was the healer of anguish, the bringer of blessedness, guide to that final blissful state so much desired by a suffering world.

This demanded a response unique in every way. But once this devotion was given, it led to an exaltation of Buddha even beyond the original conception of him. As he was no ordinary mortal, so the story of his life could not be told in ordinary human language. He could not be spoken of as others are spoken of; or, if spoken of in human language, it must be through myth and symbol and exaggerated, ecstatic expressions that expand language beyond itself and enable it to indicate by emotional intensity what it cannot clearly express. Thus the conception of Buddha, under the impulse of devotional fervour, is itself transformed. The ordinary aspect of his life is dimmed. His historical existence is considered to be only appearance. From an inspired spiritual teacher he is transformed into a divine presence.

The devotional life of Buddhism that brought about all these changes found its most powerful expression among the laity rather than among the monks. Unable to follow the severe meditative discipline prescribed for the monks, the layfolk developed a greater appreciation of the compassionate aspect of the Buddha personality. The deliverance sought by man must be something not entirely dependent on those techniques of mental concentration that cannot be learned or practised by mankind generally. Loving devotion, if it could not establish the laity in the highest stages of perfection claimed by the monks, could at least advance them on the way to release from sorrow. Much later this devotion to Buddha was to attain a certain primacy in achieving salvation. Yet even from the beginning there was a deep feeling among the followers of Buddha that devotion to the person of Buddha was essential to all who would enter on the true way of perfection.

This is shown in the very beginning of Buddhism in the formula pronounced by all those entering the community: "I go for refuge to Buddha." This is the first of the threefold commitment to Buddha, his Teaching, his Community. This formula is more devotional than legalistic, although it has both aspects. Taking refuge in Buddha indicates an attitude of spiritual dependence on Buddha as the main principle of salvation. On the part of Buddha it indicates a merciful attitude and the capacity to shelter mankind from the destructive forces at work in human life.

The followers of Buddha experienced him as the most sublime expression of reality that had come within their range of understanding. The moral, spiritual, intellectual, and emotional qualities they found in him were so sublime that they raised him above the natural and human worlds, even above the world of preternatural spirits and minor deities in the world-concept of the people. Thus Buddha became progressively identified with the final supreme reality itself.

The response to Buddha was the response of the human heart to fundamental goodness. Buddha had made a supreme gift to mankind, the greatest gift that could be given, a way of dealing with the sorrow of life. A worthy response required a return gift of total confidence and unstinted praise.

Thus began the building of shrines to Buddha in the form of stupas, then the carving in stone of the legends told about his life. Finally came the exciting moment, after five full centuries, when the Buddha image was first created. Shrines and images were multiplied, gifts were given, flowers and incense offered at the shrines, a worship tradition established. Innumerable stories were told of Buddha, stories that connected his life with every part of north India, which became in time a sacred Buddhaland, as we can see especially in the writings of Chinese pilgrims such as Fa-hsien and Hsüan-tsang. Wherever he went, Hsüan-tsang found that every locality, every village, along with the surrounding mountains, streams, trees, stones, all were in some manner related in legendary stories with the life of Buddha. All this began within the Hinayana Buddhist tradition. But the full glorification of Buddha came in the Mahayana tradition, which came later; it will be considered in a later chapter.

CHAPTER V

THE DOCTRINE

The same joy that expressed itself in praise and exaltation of Buddha flowed forth into similar praise of his teaching, known as *dharma*. This teaching was most often spoken of as "lovely in the beginning, lovely in the middle, and lovely at the ending" (*Maj.* i, 179). Dharma continues Buddha's own presence on earth. If the mortal body of the great teacher had dissolved, his doctrine remained to guide and accompany man on his way through life. "The Blessed One has come to an end, and it cannot be pointed out that he is here or there. But in the body of his doctrine he can, O King, be pointed out. For the doctrine was given by the Blessed One" (*Mil.* 73). Indeed the real test of those who honour Buddha is in the fulfilment of dharma. "Whoever walks uprightly in accordance with dharma—he it is that truly honours, reveres, respects, worships, and defers to the Tathagata in the perfection of worship" (*D.* iii, 138).

Many delightful expressions are used to bring out the beauty, loveliness, and strength of the doctrine taught by Buddha. After his illumination when Buddha started his journey to Benares he said: "To turn the dharma-wheel I go to the city of Kasi, beating the drum of deathlessness in a world that has become blind" (*Maj.* i, 171).

Many descriptions of dharma are taken from the natural world:

Monks, as in the last month of the rains, at harvest time when the sky is clear, without a cloud, and the sun, ascending in the firmament and driving away the darkness from the sky, shines forth, and is bright and brilliant—even so, monks, is this undertaking of dharma that is both happiness in the present as well as resulting in happiness in the future, because, having driven away the opposing tenets of the ordinary recluses and Brahmans, it shines forth and is bright and brilliant (*Maj.* i, 317).

This illumination is transferred to the person who responds to Buddha's teaching: "Lo ye! The Mendicant, however young, who strives to grasp the teaching of the Awakened One, he lights up the world, as, from a cloud released, the moon lights up the night" (*Dh.* 382).

Dharma is like the beautiful things that flower forth out of the earth. "As in the forest regions, the tree-tops blossom forth again in the first month of summer's heat—so did the Lord, for the profit of the world, proclaim his dharma that leads to Nirvana" (*Khuddakapatha,* Jewel Discourse, verse 12). As the farmer works the soil and tastes the fruit that comes forth from his planting, so the person who cultivates Buddha's way tastes "Dharma's sweetest bliss" (*Su.* 257).

A comparison of man's desire for a saving doctrine with man's hunger for food gives a forceful impression of the need that was satisfied by Buddha:

Lord, even as a man overcome by hunger and exhaustion might come upon a honey-ball; from each bit that he would taste he would get a sweet delicious flavour—even so, Lord, is a monk who is naturally able in mind: from each bit that he would examine with intuitive wisdom as to the meaning of this disquisition on dharma, he would get delight, he would get satisfaction for the mind (*Maj.* i, 114).

One of the most delightful scenes in Buddhist tradition is that when the first of the Buddhist nuns was received into the Order. At that time she said:

Reverend Ananda, just as a woman or man, young and tender in years and fond of dress, would, after washing her head, receive with both hands a garland of lotus flowers, of jasmine flowers or of some sweet-scented creeper and place

it on top of her head; even so I, sir, receive these eight
cardinal rules, never to be transgressed all my life (*An.* iv,
277).

All things seem to mirror forth some aspect of dharma
to Nagasena:

> Just as kings construct bathing tanks for their pleasure "so
> has the Tathagata constructed a bathing tank full of the ex-
> cellent waters of liberation—the bath of the good law." As
> men have medicines to cure the ailments of the body, so has
> the Buddha given us in his teaching "the ambrosial medicine
> which is able entirely to suppress all the sickness of sin."
> As kings put on their tables the best of foods, so has the
> Buddha given us "the most excellent, good, auspicious,
> delicate ambrosial food surpassing sweet, of the realization of
> the impermanence of all things" (*Mil.* 247–248).

The emotional response to the moral-spiritual teaching of
Buddha can be seen in the passages that refer to the manner
in which Buddha, in speaking to the brethren, "gladdened,
roused, incited, delighted them with talk on dharma" (*Maj.*
i, 176). This delight is such that "rapture is born of that
delight; being rapturous, his body is impassible; this being so,
joy is felt, and in consequence the mind is well-concentrated"
(*Maj.* i, 37).

If we turn from such general enthusiasm about Buddhist
teaching to the content of the doctrine, we must begin with
the five cardinal virtues of Buddhism which are generally
given in the following sequence: faith, energy, mindfulness,
concentration, wisdom. There are other listings of the virtues
found in Buddhist scriptures, but most often they begin with
faith and end with wisdom. These tend to be the two con-
stants. All spiritual good begins in faith and is completed in
wisdom.

The faith expected of members of the Buddhist community
is faith in the saving mission of Buddha, in the saving
power of his teaching, and in the saving presence of the

community which sustains belief and communicates it to the world.

In enumerating the four conditions that lead mankind to advantage in time and happiness in the world to come, we find: "Achievement in faith, achievement in virtue, achievement in charity, and achievement in wisdom" (*An*. iv, 283). Here a general emphasis is given to virtue generally and goodness to others, in between the two basic virtues of faith and wisdom that appear at the beginning and at the end.

We also find faith and wisdom placed in relation to other aspects of Buddhist teaching, this time to the entire body of truth. "Faith is the wealth that is here best for man. The following of dharma brings happiness. Truth is sweet beyond comparison. Life guided by wisdom is best, they say" (*Sn*. 182). A longer list that begins with faith and ends in wisdom reads: "Monks, there are these seven good qualities. What seven? Faith, conscientiousness, fear of blame, learning, strenuous energy, mindfulness, and wisdom" (*An*. iv, 144).

Faith immediately places man in a situation far removed from that of a person without faith. Faith is a leap from one order of things to another. It is like a leap across a river to another shore, another land, another country.

> Suppose a certain man should arrive, who, knowing exactly his own strength and power, should gird himself firmly and, with a spring, land himself firmly on the other side. Then the rest of the people, seeing him safe on the other side, would likewise cross. That is the way in which the recluse, by faith, aspires to leap, as it were by a bound, into higher things. For this has been said, O King, by the Blessed One in the *Samyutta Nikaya:*

> > By faith he crosses over the stream,
> > By earnestness the sea of life;
> > By steadfastness all grief he stills,
> > By wisdom is he purified (*Mil*. 36).

Here, in between faith and wisdom, we have a volitional emphasis.

Among the other virtues proper to Buddhism, one of the most attractive is the virtue of loving-kindness. This portrays the intimate, deeply affectionate aspect of Buddhism, an aspect that has been given less attention than it deserves. Much attention has been given to Buddhist metaphysics, to Buddhist meditative disciplines, to Buddhist art, but relatively little to the emotional life of Buddhism. This is considered of less significance, whereas it is of supreme significance for understanding both the Buddhist mystique and the influence this has had on the other areas of human life and culture.

The Discourse on Loving-Kindness, one of the spiritual treasures of mankind, came from the very depths of the Buddhist tradition. It is given in both the *Khuddakapatha* and the *Sutta Nipata*. In part it reads:

> May every creature abound
> In well-being and in peace.

> May every living being, weak or strong
> The long and the small
> The short and the medium-sized
> The mean and the great

> May every living being, seen or unseen
> Those dwelling far-off, those near-by
> Those already born, those waiting to be born
> May all attain inward peace.

> Let no one deceive another
> Let no one despise another in any situation
> Let no one from antipathy or hatred
> Wish evil to anyone at all.

> Just as a mother with her own life
> Protects her son, her only son, from hurt,
> So within your own self foster
> A limitless concern for every living creature.

> Display a heart of boundless love
> For all the world
> In all its height and depth and broad extent
> Love unrestrained, without hate or enmity.

Then as you stand or walk, sit or lie,
Until overcome by drowsiness
Devote your mind entirely to this;
It is known as living here a life divine (*Sn.* 146–151).

This deep affection for all the world was the object of special training:

> Herein, monks, you should train yourselves thus: "Neither will our minds become perverted, nor will we utter an evil speech, but kindly and compassionate will we dwell, having suffused that person with a mind of friendliness, void of hatred; and, beginning with him, we will dwell having suffused the whole world with a mind of friendliness that is far-reaching, widespread, immeasurable, without enmity, without malevolence." This is how you must train yourselves, monks (*Maj.* i, 129).

In the ninth chapter of Buddhaghosa's great work, *The Path of Purity,* there is a thorough study on how this extension of loving-kindness can be brought about gradually, beginning with a person's own dearest relatives and friends, then gradually attending the range of affection to include those towards whom we are indifferent, and finally to include those towards whom we have feelings of bitter antagonism.

By means of this virtue a person should be able to endure great abuse without feeling resentment arising in his heart.

> Wherefore, Phagguna, if anyone to thy face should abuse thee . . . if he were to strike you with fist or hurl clods of earth at you, or beat you with a stick, or give you a blow with a sword—yet must you set aside all worldly desires, all worldly considerations, and thus must you train yourself: "My heart shall be unwavering. No evil word will I send forth. I will abide compassionate of others' welfare, of kindly heart, without resentment." Thus must you train yourself, Phagguna (*Maj.* i, 124).

That the spiritual life of Buddhism is not simply a sublime ideal of faith, wisdom, and loving-kindness without deep moral foundations is clear from the profound sense of moral principle that dominates Buddhism in the depths of its stern realism. The Eightfold Path is itself undergirded by a fundamental demand for virtuous conduct. This is expressed in general terms in the most famous verse in the Buddhist canon. "Keep yourself from every evil deed; establish yourself in goodness; purify your own thoughts. This is the message of the enlightened ones" (*Dh.* 183).

Specific application of these general principles is contained in the first five precepts of Buddhist moral conduct. These forbid killing, stealing, impurity, lying, and intoxicating drink (*Khuddakapatha* ii). These five prohibitions are basic suppositions of the entire spiritual life of Buddhism. If relatively little direct mention is made of these commands it is because the main body of Buddhist teaching concerns the expression of the higher spiritual life.

These moral precepts are expressed more fully and in a positive rather than negative form in the Eightfold Path which constitutes the Middle Way of Buddhism:

> Hence, your reverences, greed is evil and ill-will is evil; for getting rid of greed and for getting rid of ill-will there is the Middle Path which, making for vision, making for knowledge, conduces to tranquility, to super-knowledge, to awakening, to Nirvana. And what, your reverences, is this Middle Path which, making for vision, making for knowledge, conduces . . . to Nirvana? It is this Noble Eightfold Path itself, that is to say, right view, right purpose, right speech, right action, right mode of livelihood, perfect effort, perfect mindfulness, perfect concentration. It is this, your reverences, that is the Middle Path which, making for vision, making for knowledge, conduces . . . to Nirvana (*Maj.* i, 15).

It is important to understand that all eight elements of this Path are to be carried out simultaneously and not successively in time, even though there is a progressive emphasis that passes from virtue, to spiritual concentration, to the highest spiritual wisdom.

These are the three basic divisions of the Eightfold Path:

virtuous conduct, concentration, and wisdom. Of the members of the Eightfold Path, virtuous conduct includes right speech, right action, and right livelihood. Concentration includes right effort, right mindfulness, and right concentration. Wisdom includes right view and right purpose. By attaining perfection in these three aspects of the Eightfold Path a person attains final release from all attachment and enters into Nirvana. Thus the verse: "Virtue, concentration, wisdom, and freedom sublime—these are the truths realized by Gotama, far-renowned" (*D.* ii, 123).

In many passages of Buddhist scriptures these three—virtue, concentration, and wisdom—are arranged together. The most complete explanation is given in the *Middle Length Discourses:*

> Friend Visakha, the three divisions are not arranged in accordance with the Noble Eightfold Path, but the Noble Eightfold Path is arranged in accordance with the three divisions. Whatever, friend Visakha, is right speech and whatever is right action and whatever is right way of living—these three are arranged in the class of virtue. And whatever is right effort and whatever is right mindfulness and whatever is right concentration—these are arranged in the class of concentration. And whatever is right view and right purpose —these are arranged in the class of wisdom (*Maj.* i, 301).

Turning now to virtue (*sila*) and its basic position in this pattern, we find that Buddhist doctrine is clear.

> Virtue is the base on which the man who's wise can train his heart, and make his wisdom grow. Thus shall the strenuous monk, undeceived, unravel all the tangled skein of life. This the base—like the great earth to men—and this the root of all increase in goodness, the starting point of all the Buddhas' teaching, virtue, that is, on which true bliss depends (*Mil.* 34).

The next step, *samadhi,* here translated as concentration, is also sometimes referred to as meditation, although it is very different from the meditative processes as these are generally known in the spiritual disciplines of the West. This program of training in mental concentration in Buddhism is a well-elaborated one, with detailed concern for the subject matter of thought and for the stages through which a person passes from the lower mental experiences to the highest type of mental release from the confinements that ordinarily limit our range of mental experience. The Buddhist program leads a person away from attachment—physical, emotional, and mental—to any aspect of the phenomenal world. Buddhaghosa is the great master of this process. His work, *The Path of Purity*, a long study of this process, is one of the most massive treatises ever structured on meditation and mental concentration. Yet the basic stages were already outlined in the early discourses of Buddha, beginning with his own experience and then giving instruction suited for others.

Of wisdom (*panna*), the last division of the Eightfold Path, there is a clear presentation by Nagasena in his conferences with King Menander. The King asked:

> What, Nagasena, is the characteristic mark of wisdom? I have already told you, O King, how cutting off, severance is its mark. And how? When wisdom springs up in the heart, O King, it dispels the darkness of ignorance, it causes the radiance of knowledge to arise, it makes the light of intelligence to shine forth, and it makes the noble truths plain. Thus does the recluse who is devoted to effort perceive with the clearest wisdom the impermanence of all beings and things, the universality of suffering, and the absence of any soul" (*Mil.* 39).

Thus, as the spiritual life of Buddhism begins with awareness of the threefold aspect of the phenomenal world—its impermanence (*anicca*), its painfulness (*dukkha*), its insubstantiality (*anatta*)—so the spiritual life ends there. This is the first awareness and final insight into reality, for when these things are finally appreciated, all attachment to this world is destroyed in its deepest roots; there is no longer any obstacle to a person's entry into the blissful experience at the end of the Path.

Any study of the dharma taught by Buddha might well end with consideration of the place of human effort in Buddhist spiritual discipline. Here especially we find a vigorous moral effort presented as fundamental to any spiritual achievement. As joy in the discovery of a way of salvation was so intense in Buddhism, as it had such a deeply human affection for others, as it structured the moral life so well in its essentials, so also it had an admirable emphasis on the need for a moral-spiritual effort on the part of its followers. This explains in large part Buddha's opposition to the fatalism of Gosala, the famed leader of the Ajivakas during the time of Buddha. As Buddha answered Jain extremism by insisting on the Middle Path, so he answered Ajivaka fatalism by insisting on moral effort. This insistence on moral effort was also directed against those committed to ways of salvation that depended too much on ritual, superstition, or some hereditary status of holiness.

To begin with this last, Buddha often mentioned, "No one is an outcast by birth, nor is anyone a Brahman by birth; it is by deeds that a person becomes a Brahman" (*Su.* 142). The full force of Buddha's realism can be felt in the following passage:

> If it was because of indolence, my good man, that you did not do what was lovely in body, speech, and thought, they will undoubtedly do unto you, my good man, in accordance with that indolence. For this that is an evil deed is yours; it was not done by mother, it was not done by father, it was not done by brother, it was not done by sister, it was not done by friends and acquaintances, it was not done by kith and kin, it was not done by recluses and Brahmans, it was not done by devatas. This evil deed was done by you; it is you yourself that will experience its ripening (*Maj.* iii, 179–180).

There is also the connection of deeds with each other. A person who acts must inevitably suffer the consequences of his act. "Deeds are one's own, Brahman youth, beings are heirs to deed, deeds are matrix, deeds are kin, deeds are arbiters. Deed divides beings, that is to say, by lowness and excellence" (*Maj.* iii, 203). This principle has received picturesque but powerful expression in the opening verses of the *Dhammapada,* one of the most beautiful of all Buddhist scriptures:

> All that we are is the result of what we have thought; it is founded on our thoughts, it is made up of our thoughts. If a man speaks or acts with an evil thought, pain follows him, as the wheel follows the foot of the ox that draws the carriage. All that we are is the result of what we have thought; it is founded on our thoughts, it is made up of our thoughts. If a man speaks or acts with a pure thought, happiness follows him, like a shadow that never leaves him (*Dh.* 1–2).

This inescapable determination that a man gives himself in his deepest being by his own thoughts and deeds leads to that constant exhortation of Buddhism: "Be steadfast in resolve! Watch over your own hearts! He who wearies not, but holds fast to this truth and law, shall cross this sea of life, shall make an end of grief" (*D.* ii, 120).

There are a number of words used to express this earnestness and effort that mark the spiritual life of Buddhism. The sixth member of the Eightfold Path is "right effort." The word used here is *vayamo,* sometimes translated as right endeavour. Another word frequently used is *viriya,* which means vigour, energy, effort, exertion. *Viriya* is used in the following passage. "Wherefore do you monks stir up energy to a still greater degree for attaining the unattained, for winning what is not yet won, for realizing the unrealized" (*Maj.* iii, 79). Other words are also used: *padhana,* which means exertion, striving, concentration of mind; *utthana* which means rising, getting up, rousing, energy, zeal, manly vigour, industry.

CHAPTER VI

THE COMMUNITY

The third of the Three Jewels of Buddhism, along with the person of Buddha and his teaching, is the spiritual community that he founded, the *sangha*. This community in its fullest extent was formed of both monks and lay persons. Each of these in turn was divided into a further grouping of its men and women members. The total community was formed of monks, nuns, laymen and laywomen. All lay persons in Buddhism can be considered to belong to the Buddhist religious community in somewhat the same manner as third-order associates of religious orders in the West; for all Buddhists are, in a sense, members associated in an intensive religious dedication to a specific spiritual discipline.

Yet the distinctive development of Buddhism, especially in its earlier period, is associated with the mendicant community which lived out the ascetic discipline of the *Patimokkha,* the disciplinary code of the sangha. First adopted by the mendicant community, it was later adapted to the monastic settlements. The community with its disciplinary code established the context in which the Buddhist ideal of perfection could be attained in well-graded stages of spiritual training. The community was the matrix of Buddhist holiness. Within its discipline those who had gone forth into the homeless life could live in that detachment needed for the highest mental concentration and for final attainment of Nirvana. Even the great moral values of Buddhism could not, in lay life, lead men to the stage of perfection associated with the title "Arhat." For this, a complete detachment from the ordinary life of the householder was required.

Yet this must not be taken as an indication that Buddha limited his concern to those who would formally take up the ascetic regime of the recluse. He is constantly presented in Buddhist scriptures as the universal teacher, as bringing a new form of life to all people—to the manyfolk, the *bahujana*. His way was open to all. Everyone could enter. Even in his solitude he is presented as having an irresistible attraction for the people. "He chooses a secluded lodging in a forest, at the root of a tree, on a mountain slope, in a wilderness, a hill-cave, a cemetery, a forest-haunt, in the open air or on a heap of straw. While he is living remote like this Brahman householders crowd in on him and townsfolk as well as countryfolk" (*Maj.* iii, 116).

Buddha was so concerned for the welfare of the people that he sent his closest followers on a mission to the people. "Go forth, O monks, on your wanderings, for the good of the Many—for the happiness of the Many, in compassion for the world—for the good, for the welfare, for the happiness of gods and men. Let not two of you go the same way. O monks, proclaim that teaching that is gracious at the beginning, at the middle, and at the end (*Mahavagga* I, ii, 1).

Yet the ideal of Buddhism during its early period remained that of the recluse, the *samana,* the one who had gone forth into the homeless life. The recluse of early Buddhism is described by Nagasena:

> The recluse, O King, is content with little, joyful in heart, detached from the world, apart from society, earnest in zeal, without a home, without a dwelling-place, righteous in conduct, in action without guile, skilled in duty and in the attainments—that is why whatsoever may lie before him yet to do, that can he accomplish straightway, without delay—just as the flight of your javelin, O King, is rapid because it is of pure metal, smooth, and burnished, and straight, and without a stain (*Mil.* 244).

In another list of the personal qualities of the *samana* we find self-control, virtuous conduct, calm manners, discipline of senses, patience, sympathy, love of solitude, a meditative mind, modesty and fear of doing wrong, zeal, earnestness, recitation of the scriptures, rejoicing in goodness, and freedom of attachment (*Mil.* 162). These qualities were found in all the true recluses of the period.

The going forth into the homeless life was not unique with the followers of Buddha. He did not invent this way of life. It had already emerged from within the primordial spiritual traditions of India itself. It was pre-Aryan, or at least non-Aryan, in origin. If this way of life is found also in the Brahmanical tradition of India, it was absorbed into it after the Aryan-Sanskrit-Vedic tradition had been brought into India and had been profoundly influenced by spiritual forces already at work there. At the time of Buddha those living the homeless life were already accepted among the people as having a recognized social status. In them was manifest the heroic effort made in India, not only to rise mentally to the highest intellectual experience of the reality beyond all names and forms, but also to divest life itself of all its encumbrances, even those of a religious and sacramental order, for in the final stages of perfection these too must be abandoned. In the Brahmanical tradition this required that the sacred thread itself be buried, that the sacrificial fire be extinguished, that the sacred vessels be symbolically destroyed.

Thus out of the Brahmanical and the non-Brahmanical traditions of India a class of sacred persons was created that lived with no possessions except robe, staff, and begging bowl. To beg food for life was considered one of the noblest human, religious, and spiritual acts. In a corresponding way the giving of alms to these persons was a deed of exceptional merit for lay persons.

Buddha himself emerged out of this class of persons. As a boy he had met them often in his native place. When he became aware of the sorrow of life and wished to live on a higher spiritual plane, it was natural that he should go for guidance to two recluses, Alara Kalama and Uddakha Rajaputta. Later his first followers were from this class. The original group that he formed was not unlike the other groups of mendicants following other spiritual leaders of his time, men such as Purana Kassapa, Mokkhali Gosala, Pakudha Kaccana, Nigantha Nayaputta, Ajita Keskambali, and Sanjaya Balatthiputta, to mention only the more important of those known to us. Of these the Jains and the Ajivakas are most often mentioned in early Buddhist writings.

What was unique with Buddha was his capacity to form an effective community of his followers, a community that would perpetuate itself, expand its membership, preserve his teaching and commit it to writing, provide spiritual guidance for the people, establish permanent monastic centres, develop the higher mystical and metaphysical implications of the doctrine, create an art suited to the devotional lives of the people, and carry his teaching to distant lands throughout the Far East until it gave that vast region and its peoples their greatest single bond of spiritual, intellectual, religious, and artistic culture.

During the lifetime of Buddha, the community established by him had no permanent dwelling place. Wandering ascetics, they met and stayed together only during the three months of the rainy season. Buddha himself provided the unity of the group. He was present to solve all disputes and to identify the correct teaching. More than that, he was a kind of saviour-guide about whom the group gathered. His personality radiated so powerfully over the community that later the community felt it could establish no regulation without invoking some legendary incident according to which the regulation was sanctioned by Buddha himself.

It is clear from the early records that Buddha sought to form a community open to all who wished to enter upon a sound spiritual way of life. He sought to avoid all sectarian limitations on the teaching he imparted and the discipline he established. When he spoke of the community he referred to the Community of the Four Quarters—that is, the community in its universal extent. This included all members of the community, lay and religious. It also included an invitation of all mankind to enter the community, although he frequently spoke of attracting young men of good family— that is, persons of the higher classes—to enter the way of life that he had established.

While the unity óf the group was preserved with a certain ease during the lifetime of Buddha, a traumatic experience awaited the Order at the time of Buddha's death. This was felt the more severely because Buddha consistently refused to establish any central authority or to name any personal successor to guide the community after his death. Later Ananda was asked: "Is there, good Ananda, even one monk who was designated by the good Gotama saying: 'After my passing this one will be your support, and to him you might have recourse now?' " The answer of Ananda was, "There is not even one monk, Brahman, who was designated by the Lord who knew and saw, Perfected One, fully self-awakened one, saying: 'After my passing this one will be your support,' and to whom we might have recourse now." The further question then was, "But is there even one monk who is agreed upon by the Order?" Giving a negative answer to this, Ananda declared: "We, Brahman, are not without support; we have a support, Brahman; dharma is our support." In further extension of this idea is the statement: "Indeed the reverend ones do not deal with us, it is the dharma that deals with us" (*Maj.* iii, 9).

That Buddha established no central authority was due to his exceptional insight into the mind, emotions, and the need for freedom experienced by the mendicants of India. It also represents a superb confidence in the doctrine he taught. Yet that he established no centre of authority in the community, except the community itself gathered in assembly, remains difficult for the Western mind to understand, accustomed as it is to some instrument of authority to guide and administer every society, even religious societies.

The higher development of the monastic establishment, the sangha, was especially the work of the immediate followers of Buddha. Had they been men of less genius they would not have been able to hold together as a vital community. Disputes did arise; Buddha's only suggestion had been:

> As to this, Ananda, monks dispute, saying: "It is dharma" . or "It is not dharma" or "It is discipline" or "It is not discipline." One and all of these monks should assemble in a complete Order. Having assembled, what belongs to dharma should be discussed; having discussed what belongs to dharma according to how it corresponds here, so should that legal question be settled. And what, Ananda, is the decision of the majority? If these monks, Ananda, are not able to settle that legal question in this residence, then, Ananda, these monks must go to a residence where there are more monks, and there one and all must assemble in a complete Order (*Maj.* ii, 245).

Concerning the correct teaching there was difficulty throughout the entire course of Buddhist history. However, there was one clear instrument of unity from a very early time that kept the Buddhist monastic discipline intact and provided a basic concord in the evolving communities of monks: This instrument was the *Patimokkha,* a list of 227 monastic regulations that, in its earlier form, was the effective norm of community life at the time of Buddha's death. This was a legalistic document. Strict adherence to its prescriptions often turned Buddhist thought to legal problems rather than to essential spiritual issues. Yet this did give to the Buddhist community its basic instrument of survival as a disciplined community.

If a study of the sangha and these regulations does not have the attraction found in the study of the Buddha personality, if it does not have the satisfying splendour found in the study of Buddhist doctrine, it is nonetheless a study of supreme importance for understanding the firmest structural support of Buddhism. The entire historical development was in a way dependent on this structure. These regulations gave to Buddhism the hard earthly foundation that was necessary to sustain the Buddhist community and its doctrine, and to continue the work of the founder. The prescriptions of the *Patimokkha* and the *Vinaya* are simple, legalistic, even trivial. Yet they established a sound form of daily living for those seeking the final spiritual experience of which man is capable.

At least in its earliest form there is in the *Patimokkha* a certain majesty of conception. This early form can be seen in the *Dhammapada:* "Patience is the highest penance, Nirvana the supreme attainment, thus have the Buddhas declared: For he is not a true recluse who hurts others, nor is he a true recluse who causes sorrow to others. Restraint from all evil, accumulation of all that is good, and purification of one's own mind, this is the teaching of the Buddhas" (*Dh.* 184, 183).

The full mystique of the Buddhist community was not developed until the time of the Mahayana, a later phase of Buddhist development. But there did develop some depth of feeling for the community. This feeling of identity with the community intensified the monks' experience of faith and joy. This is expressed by Buddhaghosa:

> When a monk is devoted to this recollection of the community, he is respectful and reverential towards the community. He attains fullness of faith, has much happiness and bliss, conquers fear and dread, is able to endure pain. He comes to feel as if he were living in the presence of the community. Even his body, when the recollection of the sangha's special qualities dwells in it, becomes as worthy of veneration as an Uposatha house where the community has met. His mind tends towards the attainment of the community's special qualities. On meeting an opportunity for transgression,

his awareness and his shame are as vivid as if he were face to face with the community. If he rises no higher, he is at least advancing towards a happy end. When a man becomes truly wise his constant effort will be this recollection of the community blessed with such mighty efficacy (*Vis.* vii, 100).

[Later with more spiritual concerns Buddhaghosa writes of the sangha:] It is an incomparable field of merit for the world, a place without equal in the world for growing merit; just as the place for growing the king's or the minister's rice or corn is the king's rice-field or the king's corn-field, so the community is the place for growing the whole world's merit. For the world's various kinds of merit leading to welfare and happiness grow with the community as their support. Therefore the community is "an incomparable field of merit for the world" (*Vis.* vii, 98).

But if the monks living within monastic walls carried on the higher spiritual quest according to the teachings of Buddha and elaborated a further exposition of Buddha's doctrine, the laity also formed an essential part of the Buddhist community. They carried on their share of the teaching of Buddha and gave it an elaboration specific to themselves. In the end they may have determined the development and destiny of Buddhism to a greater extent than the monks. It was the laity that brought Buddhism into contact with the imagination, the emotions, and the piety of the people of India. From this contact much of the higher cultural development of Buddhism took place.

The laity had their own special realization of the Buddha, the dharma, the sangha. Buddha progressively became for the people an object of intense devotion and even worship. He provided their highest experience of the divine. This category, that of the divine, remained a powerful force in the lives of the people, even when it was neglected by the monks. This sense of the divine gradually merged with their deep feeling and reverence for Buddha.

Also as regards dharma, the layfolk shifted the emphasis in the Buddhist tradition from the quest for salvation through ascetic practises to a quest for salvation through faith and heavenly grace. As regards the community, the laity had originally been associated with the mendicant community from without. They were privileged to provide alms for the monks to endow the monasteries, to support the programs for building stupas. Later it became clearer to the laity that they were themselves followers of Buddha, that the way of the monks was not essential to the highest perfection, that devotion was superior to asceticism, that Budda was a much more divine person than the monks realized, and his teaching more sublime. Yet it remained true that laity and recluse were mutually dependent on each other. The relationship between monk and layfolk is described in the *Itivuttikam:*

> Remember, monks, that Brahmans and housefathers are most helpful to you, since they support you with robe and bowl, with lodging and seat, medicines and necessities in time of illness. You also, monks, are most helpful to Brahmans and housefathers, for you teach them dharma that is lovely at the beginning, lovely in the middle, and lovely at the end, both in spirit and in letter, and you proclaim to them the higher life in its completeness and utter purity. Thus, monks, this sublime life is lived in mutual dependence for ferrying across the flood, for the utter ending of ill (*Iti.* 111).

Remembrance of the community is one of the greatest blessings in Buddhist life for everyone, for the laity as well as for the monks: "As he calls to mind the Order, his mind is calmed, delight arises, the soiling of the mind is purified, just like the cleansing of a dirty garment by a proper process. . . ." (*An.* i, 208).

As the monks have their specific virtues, so also the layfolk. When the question came up in the discussions that took place between King Menander and the monk Nagasena, the answer given by Nagasena was:

> These ten, O King, are the virtues of a lay disciple:
> 1. He suffers like pain and feels like joy as the Order does.
> 2. He takes the dharma as his master.

3. He delights in giving so far as he is able to give.
4. On seeing the dharma of the Conqueror decay, he does his best to revive it.
5. He holds right views.
6. Having no passion for excitement, he runs not after any other teacher his life long.
7. He keeps a guard over himself in thought and deed.
8. He delights in peace, is a lover of peace.
9. He feels no jealousy and walks not in religion in a quarrelsome spirit.
10. He takes his refuge in the Buddha; he takes his refuge in dharma; he takes his refuge in the Order (*Mil.* 94).

Another list of lay virtues enumerates eight things that should be given up by the true lay disciple of Buddha: onslaught on creatures, taking what is not given, lying speech, slanderous speech, covetousness and greed, angry faultfinding, wrathful rage, arrogance (*Maj.* i, 287). Here the sense of noninjury to others, whether in deed or in thought or emotional antagonism, dominates the entire attitude that is presented.

Yet another list takes up the threefold aspect of human moral conduct, that which concerns body, speech, and thought. In body there is to be restraint in injury to creatures, no taking of what is not given, no involvement in deeds of lust. In speech there is to be no lying, no slanderous speech, no harsh speech, no frivolous chatter. In thought there is to be nothing covetous, nothing malevolent, no wrong view of things, no perverted outlook (*Maj.* i, 287–289).

CHAPTER VII

SECT AND SCHISM

Buddhism, as any vital spiritual or intellectual tradition, felt within itself certain tensions from a very early period. These tensions existed within an undivided community during the lifetime of Buddha and for some hundred years after his death. But gradually the differences of thought and spiritual experience within the community came to express themselves in the establishment of diverse sects or schools of thought. Each claimed to be heir of traditions handed down from the beginning.

An understanding of these schools of thought is especially important in Buddhism because the original tradition has come down to us only in these diverse schools. When we first come across differences of interpretation of Buddhist teaching we tend to be somewhat confused until we learn to deal with Buddhism not as a single tradition fixed from the beginning, but as a differentiated tradition in a state of continual change, development, and apparent contradiction. This is especially true of the first six hundred years of Buddhist development in India.

In its entire history the greatest single difference that developed within Buddhism is the difference between Mahayana and Hinayana forms of Buddhism, meaning the Buddhism of the Great Vehicle and the Buddhism of the Small Vehicle. These names, which have been generally accepted since the beginning of the Christian era, were given by the defenders of the Mahayana tradition, which assumed a superior position. There was a vast difference and yet a close relationship between the two traditions. Within both of these traditions a number of other, subordinate schools of thought developed. Within the Hinayana over twenty divisions are mentioned in Buddhist writings, although most often there is mention of eighteen schools. This later became the standard number used in designating the multiple schools of the Hinayana. Yet of this number only some five or six are of great significance. Even these can, for our immediate purpose, be reduced to three: the Theravada, the Mahasanghika, and the Sarvastivada. In the present chapter, we are concerned only with these schools of the Hinayana Buddhism. The Mahayana brought about such a basic transformation in Buddhism that it must be treated separately.

The greatest and most significant division of Hinayana Buddhism was the division between the Theravada and Mahasanghika. These two terms mean the Doctrine of the Ancients and the Doctrine of the Great Council. The division between these two did not emerge in fully developed form until the third century B.C., after some two centuries of Buddhist growth and expansion. Yet the division had its deepest roots in the period of Buddha himself. So important is this division that the entire history of Buddhism can, and even must, be told in terms of it. It is known in Buddhist history as the Great Schism. Asked to explain the conflict that brought about this division we would answer that it was a conflict between the more rigid, rational, and clerical dominated type of Buddhism and a less rigid, more devotional, lay-orientated type of Buddhism.

Of Buddha himself it could be said that he was such an amazing spiritual master that he kept these two forces under harmonious control during his lifetime. To some extent his leading disciple, Shariputra, was the stricter personality, supporting the earliest tendency towards rigidity in discipline and doctrine. Yet some foundations for strict interpretation can be found in the teaching and the actions of Buddha himself. Apparently Buddha gave most of his time to the monks.

He gave much less time to the lay people. At least this seems
to have been the case from a thorough reading of the early
documents that come down to us. Yet we must always remem-
ber that the documents come down to us through the monks,
and thus consciously or unconsciously they may have given
us a very limited view of the real teachings and actions of
Buddha. But as we have no other sources to go on, we can
only say that according to the records as we possess them,
there was a very early emphasis on the mendicant life, on
the spiritual development of the monks, and on the inescapable need for human effort in attaining salvation. Yet
strangely enough, even while Buddha was insisting on the
need for self-reliance in the spiritual life of man, he was
himself providing in his own person, his own teaching, and
his own example an extrinsic aid that did not well fit into
the system that he was teaching. Again it could be said
that he gave a strongly rationalist foundation to his spiritual
discipline. He carefully avoided the miraculous, the super-
stitious, the quest for heavenly aid.

It must also be said that Buddha constantly sought to avoid
controversy. One of the most famous of all the passages of
Buddhist scriptures is the passage addressed to Malunkyaputta:

> Whoever, Malunkyaputta, should speak thus: "I will not
> fare the Brahma-faring under the Lord until the Lord ex-
> plains to me whether the world is eternal or whether the
> world is not eternal . . . or whether the Tathagata neither
> is nor is not after dying"—this man might pass away,
> Malunkyaputta, before this was explained to him by the
> Tathagata. Malunkyaputta, it is as if a man were pierced by
> an arrow thickly smeared with poison and his friends and
> relations, his kith and kin, were to procure a physician and
> surgeon. He might say: "I will not draw out this arrow until
> I know whether this man who pierced me is a noble or Brahman
> or merchant or worker." . . . He might speak thus: "I
> will not draw out this arrow until I know the name and clan
> of the man who pierced me." He might speak thus: "I will

not draw out this arrow until I know whether the man who pierced me is tall or short or middling in height." . . . Malunkyaputta, this man might pass away before this was known to him. In the same way, Malunkyaputta, whoever should say, "I will not fare the Brahma-faring under the Lord until he explains to me either that the world is eternal or that the world is not eternal . . . or that the Tathagata neither is nor is not after dying"—this man might pass away, Malunkyaputta, before it was explained to him by the Tathagata.

This living of the Brahma-faring, Malunkyaputta, could not be said to depend on the view that the world is eternal. Nor could the living of the Brahma-faring, Malunkyaputta, be said to depend on the view that the world is not eternal. Whichever view is correct, whether the world is eternal or not eternal, there is birth, there is aging, there is dying, there are grief, sorrow, suffering, lamentation and despair, the suppression of which I lay down here and now" (*Maj.* i, 428–430).

Thus Buddha only put off to a future date the more severe intellectual conflicts that were inherent in the doctrines he was teaching. Buddha was exceptionally clear on precisely what he did not wish to explain and precisely what he did wish to explain. As regards what he did wish to explain, he said:

What has been explained by me, Malunkyaputta? "This is anguish" has been explained by me, Malunkyaputta. "This is the arising of anguish; this is the stopping of anguish; this is the path leading to the stopping of anguish"—these have been explained by me. And why? Because it is connected with the goal, is fundamental to the Brahma-faring, and conduces to turning away from, to dispassion, stopping, calming, super-knowledge, awakening and Nirvana. Wherefore, Malunkyaputta, understand as not explained what has not been explained by me (*Maj.* i, 431–432).

Buddha considered the great dilemmas of reality as beyond resolution by the human intelligence. They were, he thought, best left aside. There was only the Middle Path between eternalism and nihilism, future existence and extinction, ascetic severity and overindulgence. Of these problems inherent in the teaching bequeathed to his followers, it was the moral and disciplinary problems that first came to the fore.

In the same year of Buddha's death in 486, Kassapa, leading Arhat of the community, called a council in which certain questions of doctrine and of monastic discipline were settled. This council is known as the Council of Rajagriha, the first of the three early councils mentioned in Buddhist scriptures. Just what doctrines were discussed we do not know. At a later period it was thought that the entire canon of Buddhist scriptures had first been recited at this meeting. This was obviously impossible. As regards discipline, the central point of discussion was the strictness with which the regulations of the mendicant community should be enforced. According to Ananda, Buddha, before his death, had declared that the minor elements of the rule could be changed but that the major elements should remain unchanged. Although this was reported to the council, the decision made was to keep the rules just as they were, since Buddha had failed to identify which were the greater and which were the lesser.

Of much more significance at this first council was the fact that the Arhats assumed control of the Order. This eventually proved the source of greatest tension. From this time on, decisions were made both in doctrine and in discipline that favoured the Arhats—that is, the monks of highest spiritual attainment—over the rest of the Buddhist community. Thus began the clerical domination of Buddhist life and thought. According to their teaching, perfection and entry into Nirvana required that a person go forth from the homeless life into the status of a recluse and follow the established discipline until he attained the perfection of the Arhat. This left the laity in a very subordinate spiritual position in the community. Their role was limited to supporting the monks, keeping the basic moral code, and following the decisions made for them. It also failed to recognize the high spiritual value of faith and devotion as a way of salvation.

At the next council, that of Vaisali, held in 386, a hundred years after the Council of Rajagriha, the main points of discussion were certain monastic regulations concerning customs of eating, administration of the monastery, and possessions that were permitted to the monks. The decisions made at this time were again in favor of the more strict interpretation of tradition. Dogmatic and disciplinary legalism was progressively taking control of the community.

According to some records, especially *The Chronicle of Ceylon,* this was the moment, after the Council of Vaisali, when the fundamental division took place between the Theravada and the Mahasanghika traditions. Vasumitra also places the division a few years after this council. But whether or not the Great Schism occurred so soon after this second council, it certainly developed during the period between the second and the third council, that of Pataliputra, held in the reign of Asoka in 256 B.C.

It is not certainly known whether or not this Council of Pataliputra ever took place, or if it did take place, precisely what was its nature, who was there, how was it conducted, what were its decisions. There is little information on the council in the Buddhist writings. The work supposedly written just after this council, *The Points of Controversy,* was certainly composed some three centuries later. Yet in Buddhist tradition so much happened at this time that we must consider that a serious meeting did take place, that serious decisions were made which further confirmed the divisions that were developing within Buddhist thought and discipline. According to one of the most important works in the later Buddhist writings, the work called *The Great Commentary,* a series of five propositions was set forth by the monk Mahadeva.

These propositions stated: 1. Arhats were subject to sexual temptation and at least to some forms of involuntary physical impurity. 2. Arhats were subject to some forms of ignorance. 3. Arhats were subject to doubt. 4. Arhats could be instructed by others. 5. Entry into the first stages of higher mental concentration was accompanied by a vocal outcry.

While these appear to be quite simple and nonincriminatory, they were resented by the Arhats and were condemned at the council. Indeed this constituted the first serious challenge to the status of the Arhats. It brought them closer to the ordinary Buddhist devotee and brought the ordinary Buddhist closer to the status of perfection by diminishing the distance between the two.

Later, all of this discussion and the controversies that took place at this time were dealt with in an extensive work, *The Points of Controversy*. In this work, over five hundred propositions associated with some twenty different schools of Hinayana Buddhism were presented for discussion and resolution according to the Theravada tradition, which, during the last two centuries in the pre-Christian era, established itself as the major Buddhist tradition of southern India and Ceylon. From this time on, the issues were fairly joined. All Buddhist development since the time of Asoka must be seen in terms of the different schools of Buddhism that emerged from this original division. Passing now to a discussion of the three major schools of Hinayana Buddhism, we consider first the Theravada, then the Mahasanghika and the Sarvastivada.

The Theravada, which kept a certain continuity from the time of Buddha, can be said to represent the more rigorous and perhaps the more orthodox of these three traditions. The Theravada held firm to the original discipline and to the rational-contemplative aspect of the doctrine. Its followers kept the doctrine that final spiritual liberation of man required a going forth from the status of householder into the homeless state; that Buddha was a real human person though with unique status and with a universal mission to mankind; that the elements that constitute reality are real even though this reality is only a succession of momentary existence. The Theravada were in general adverse to the expansion of the devotional attitude that developed within the other schools. In particular they were opposed to the elevation of Buddha to divine status.

The Theravada constitute a large section of Buddhism as it exists in the present time. It is sometimes referred to as Southern Buddhism to distinguish it from the Mahayana Buddhism that flourished more in the north of India and which spread on into central and eastern Asia. Theravada Buddhism established itself most firmly in Ceylon, Burma, Thailand, Laos, and Cambodia. Because Theravada Buddhism is the only form of Hinayana Buddhism that survives on any extensive scale there is a tendency to identify Theravada Buddhism with Hinayana Buddhism. Yet it must be remembered that the Theravada is only one of many schools of Hinayana Buddhism that once existed.

The greatest of the Theravada teachers is Buddhaghosa, who produced a massive amount of writing both in the form of commentaries on the Sutras and in the form of original works of his own. His great synthesis, the masterwork of Theravada thought, is the *Path of Purity*.

A number of sects were derived from the Theravadins. They were the Sarvastivadins, the Vibhajyavadins, the Mahisakas, the Dharmaguptas. Of these, the Sarvastivadins and the sects derived from the Sarvastivadins are most important.

The next school of Buddhist development that is of supreme importance for understanding both the doctrinal structure and the historical development of Buddhism is the Mahasanghika. It was the followers of this tradition that caused the deepest inner ferment of Buddhism during the last two centuries of the pre-Christian period and the first few centuries of the Christian period. From this school of Buddhism developed those currents of thought that inclined towards the exaltation of Buddha as a transterrestrial being who came to earth as appearance and not as reality. This school accepted miraculous events with ease and inclined more to the devotional than to the ascetic forms of sanctity; it was also more concerned with the salvation of the people generally than with the salvation of the monks.

The Mahasanghika was also distinctive in its capacity for evolving a deep cultural communication between Buddhism and the religious conceptions of the people. Because it understood the popular forms of piety and of folk art, the Mahasanghika established itself on a more popular basis than the other Hinayana schools.

But if there was in the Mahasanghika tradition this emphasis on devotion there was also in the Mahasanghika tradition a new depth of metaphysical insight. This was manifested particularly in the development given to the *sunyata* concept that had been in the Buddhist tradition from the beginning but which had thus far not been developed. Until the time of the Mahasanghika, the capacity to dwell mentally in the realm of emptiness, or *sunyata,* was only one of the capacities developed in the successive stages of mental concentration. Its real metaphysical implications came only with this new development that took place under the Mahasanghika. It was from this beginning that the concept of emptiness was developed, first in the wisdom literature of the Mahayana tradition, and later by Nagarjuna. The concept of *sunyata* became the central concept of the Madhyamika tradition of Buddhist thought, the most powerful thought system evolved in the entire history of Buddhism.

Of the Mahasanghika scriptures the most significant work that has survived is the *Mahavastu,* an extensive life of Buddha, written in Sanskrit, which was discovered in Nepal.

In the wider story of Buddhism, the Mahasanghika is most significant for the part it played in preparing the way for the Mahayana development. Indeed, the Mahasanghika school did not survive after the decline of Buddhism in India at the end of the first millennium A.D. But its essential teachings were taken up and further expanded and carried far across the Asian world by the Mahayana.

If we turn now to Sarvastivada, we find that this was one of several traditions that derived from the Theravada. We know the teaching of the Sarvastivadins with some thoroughness because it has the most extensive scriptures and commentaries of any Hinayana school other than the Theravada. The great commentaries, the *Vibhasa* and the *Mahavibhasa*, composed by Sarvastivadin writers on the doctrinal sections of Buddhist scriptures, are especially valuable. These commentaries, in turn, formed the basis for the extensive synthesis written by Vasubandhu under the title of *Abhidharmakosa*, the greatest synthesis created in any of the Hinayana schools. It is to the Sarvastivadins what the *Visuddhimagga,* the *Path of Purity,* is to the Theravada.

The Sarvastivadins maintained that all the component elements of reality, that is, all the dharmas, are real and continue to extend their existence from the past into the future. The composite realities that result from these dharmas have only transient existence. Yet there is a certain type of reality, that of the dharmas, that can be associated with past, present, and future. In this manner the Sarvastivadins tried to expound a doctrine that would satisfy the need for explaining both change and continuity in things. The name "Sarvastivada" means "The doctrine that all things exist."

A number of schools of thought emerged from the Sarvastivada; each of these gave to this trend of thought an extensive enrichment. Of these schools the most significant are the Vatsiputrya, the Sammatiya, the Mahisasaka, the Dharmaguptaka, and the Sautrantika. The intensity of thought that these various schools gave to the basic metaphysical problems of reality, to analysis of the psychical world, to the problems of causality, to the nature of existing things, to the knowledge process, was very great.

Thus we end with an extensive variety of sects and schools within Buddhism. Because of this, Buddhism has become

one of the most difficult of all thought traditions to understand. It is especially difficult because the records as we
possess them today are incomplete. Only the Theravada and
the Sarvastivada have left a sizable amount of scriptural
writing. Each of these two sects has also left us with masterful commentaries, studies, and an outstanding synthesis, all
of which are wonderfully helpful in our study.

While these two sects have left us with extensive material
and a synthesis, none of the other schools have left us with
any extensive scriptures, commentaries, studies, or any final
synthesis. Thus there is much about the earlier period that
we cannot adequately study.

But while there is a wide diversity of thought traditions
within Buddhism there is also a surprising unity that becomes increasingly clear the better one is acquainted with
the writings of the different schools. In studying Buddhism a
certain dialectical process can be observed. First the student
experiences a sense of unity in Buddhism, a unity that is
clearly visible when Buddhism is set against the other spiritual traditions of mankind. Then the student learns something of the diversity within Buddhism. At this time the
unity of the tradition seems to dissolve, especially the unity
between the Hinayana and Mahayana forms of Buddhism.
Then, finally, after attaining a thorough understanding of the
various schools of Buddhist thought, both Hinayana and
Mahayana, the student has a new and more profound experience of the basic unity that underlies all forms of Buddhism and binds them together within the one tradition.

The range of discourse and its terms are common to all
the Buddhist schools and to no other thought tradition. All
are working on problems that emerge from the same basic
thought experience. The diversity that emerges is itself extremely fruitful, for the elucidation offered by the whole
diversified tradition is much greater than what could be offered by any single tradition. Diversity is seen as enrichment,
not as impoverishment, as illumination rather than con-

fusion, a desirable complexity rather than contradiction. It gave to the entire process of Buddhist development an intensely felt spiritual and intellectual dynamic.

As a final word about the work of these schools of Buddhist thought, we note that these schools were the instruments not merely for a vital intellectual effort within Buddhism; they also provided the context within which the great literary, artistic, and missionary work of Buddhism was carried out. The different schools set up the monasteries and eventually gave to Buddhist intellectual life an academic context in which the doctrines could be studied and permanent traditions established. It was in the settlements of these different schools of thought that the great scriptures of Buddhism were written down in the early centuries of the Christian era.

CHAPTER VIII

THE SCRIPTURES

Along with the establishment of the monastic life and the development of the different schools of Buddhist thought, a third, most significant, development was the composition of the Buddhist scriptures. An effort to identify the correct doctrines taught by Buddha and to fix in permanent form their precise verbal expression was made just after his death. The beginning of this work is generally ascribed to the first council held at Rajagriha in 486. Later generations thought that the whole of the disciplinary and doctrinal scriptures of Buddhism were recited and fixed at the time of this council. This is certainly not true. What is true is that a beginning was made at that time to clarify and preserve the essentials of Buddha's discourses.

This work was carried on by an oral tradition for over four hundred years. An elaboration of Buddha's teaching was taking place at the same time when the text of his teaching was being established. Thus in the texts, as they were later written down, there are elements that cover several centuries of development. Our best way of identifying the earliest forms of the scriptural texts is by the agreement between the Pali canon of the Theravada tradition and the canon of the Sarvastivada tradition that is preserved in Chinese translation. From a general agreement in these different traditions we can come to some idea of the earlier form of some of the major texts. Agreement between texts indicates that the work was received by the different schools from a single earlier tradition that was adopted by both.

The basic texts of the Hinayana tradition were probably established in their essential outlines within two centuries after the time of Buddha, probably by the middle of the third century B.C. These scriptures were handed down by schools of reciters who carefully memorized the text word for word and spoke the text publicly for the benefit of the others. After the time of Asoka the various schools of Hinayana Buddhism were the centres for passing on the texts. These had a certain fundamental identity, as we can see by comparison of the Sarvastivada canon as preserved in the Chinese language with the Theravada canon as preserved in the Pali language.

Because several schools of Buddhist thought existed at this time, and the scriptures were preserved within these schools, the sacred texts acquired over the course of several centuries a certain differentiation of expression and development. Thus we have a number of different traditions in the handing down of the canons of Buddhist scriptures, all slightly different from each other and written in different languages.

At present we know of four collections of Buddhist scriptures: three of these belong to Hinayana Buddhism, the fourth to Mahayana.

1. The Theravada collection, written in the Pali language, is the only complete Buddhist canon to survive until our own times. It was preserved in Ceylon and in the countries of southeast Asia.

2. The Sarvastivada collection, written originally in Sanskrit. Most of the Sanskrit texts have disappeared, but the texts themselves survive in Chinese and Tibetan translations.

3. The Mahasanghika collection, written originally in Sanskrit and preserved in the Lokottaravada school. Of this tradition we have only the Sanskrit text of the *Mahavastu* and a few other fragments. The rest of the Mahasanghika writings have disappeared.

4. The Mahayana collection contains an extensive list of writings, although there is no separate Mahayana canon with such definitive status as the Pali canon of the Theravada. The Mahayana scriptures were composed much later and with greater preoccupation both for metaphysical insight into reality and for the devotional way of salvation.

Since the Theravada Pali canon is our only complete canon, it deserves extensive consideration by everyone with any basic interest in Buddhist doctrines. The canon is divided into three sections: 1. The *Vinaya* or *Disciplinary Section*. 2. The *Sutra* or *Doctrinal Section*. 3. The *Abhidharma Section*, which contains analytical studies of the doctrinal portions of the scriptures.

1. *The Disciplinary Section* gives the basic rules for monastic life. This section contains first the *Sutta-Vibhanga*, which prescribes the basic regime of the Buddhist community of monks. Each of the 227 fundamental rules known as the *Patimokkha* is given in the *Sutta-Vibhanga* along with an account of how the rule came to be made and how it was sanctioned by Buddha himself.

The *Disciplinary Section* also contains a second division which in turn is divided into the Great Series and Small Series of rules for dealing with special aspects of monastic life. The Great Series gives the rules for admission to the Order, the days for meeting in the Uposatha ceremony and for the ritual recital of the *Patimokkha*. It also contains the laws governing the residence of the monks during the rainy season; rules for the use of leather for shoes or dress and for furniture; rules for medicine, for making and distributing robes, for official processes in case of dissension within the monastery.

The Small Series gives the rules for dealing with offences, for reconciliation of monks who have been punished, for dealing with schism, along with the rules for the ordination and instruction of nuns. There is also in this series, at the end, a very important historical section that narrates the history of the first Council at Rajagriha and also the second Council at Vaisali.

2. *The Sutra Section* contains the most important material for the study of Buddhist doctrine. It is composed primarily of the discourses of Buddha. These discourses are gathered into five divisions. The first four divisions are made according to the length of the discourses or according to their relation to each other. Thus we have (1) The Long Discourses, (2) The Medium Length Discourses, (3) The Kindred Sayings, (4) The Gradual Discourses. To these four a fifth collection, The Short Treatises, is added of those accounts of Buddha's teaching which were not included in the previous collections. Thus there are, all together, five collections of Sutras.

The Collection of Long Discourses contains 34 Sutras arranged in three series. The first series, which includes the first 13 discourses, is known as the Division of Moral Rules. The second series, known as the Great Series, consists of Sutras 14 to 23. This series contains a number of Sutras of exceptional importance in the expression of Buddhist teaching. There is first of all, the *Story of the Great Decease,* the account of Buddha's last days, his last teaching, and his death. This Sutra contains a summary of the most significant of Buddha's teaching and has always had a special place in the Buddhist scriptures. It has supplied a number of motifs for Buddhist iconography. Two other Sutras of this series are concerned with the last days of Buddha—the *Great King of Glory Sutra* and the *Jana-Vasabha Story.* Of still greater importance for Buddhist teaching is the *Great Discourse on Causation.* This Sutra deals with the central doctrine of Buddhism, which is that of causation and the manner in which ignorance and desire arise in man. Once this analysis is made, then the manner of attaining liberation is clearly seen. Also in this series we find the *Setting-Up of Mindful-*

ness Sutra, which explains the good effect of constant inner awareness of the true reality of things. Gradually through this mindfulness, all desire is extinguished and the monk attains Nirvana.

The third division of the Long Sutras contains Sutras 24 to 34. Of these Sutras, one of special significance is the *Discourse Given to Sigala,* a discourse giving spiritual instruction to a layman to guide him in his conduct in the world.

The Middle Length Discourses are constituted of 152 Sutras in fifteen different series. This collection, exceptionally rich in doctrinal content, is too diverse to outline in detail. For special mention we might choose Sutra 26, *The Noble Quest.* In this Sutra we have one of the finest outlines of the life of Buddha and his quest for enlightenment. Also there are Sutras 121 and 122 on emptiness. These begin a thorough presentation of the mental awareness of the nonconceptual aspect of reality that later became such an important aspect of Buddhist thought. In addition to these there is the short but very significant Sutra, *The Lesser Discourse to Malunkya.* This contains the direct statement of Buddha's desire to avoid speculative questions in favour of discussion concerning things immediately profitable for the life of virtue and for that concentration of mind which is needed for the attainment of Nirvana.

The third collection of Sutras, The Kindred Sayings, is composed of Sutras that are grouped very loosely into five series. They are generally of less importance than those of the first two collections, the Long and the Medium Length Discourses.

The fourth collection, The Gradual Sayings, is composed of sayings that are grouped into eleven series. The first series contains the one form, the one scent, the one hindrance, etc. The second series has the two faults, the two powers, the two fools, etc. Within this context many significant things are said which resolve many points of Buddhist doctrine and are of great aid in clarifying teaching that is inadequately presented in other parts of the scriptures

There is, finally, the fifth collection, the Collection of Short Treatises. This collection, which was made after the other collections of Sutras were substantially complete, includes many texts of exceptional value. Some come down from a very early period. They tend to have a conciseness and a maturity of statement that make them especially valuable for the Western reader who is for the first time becoming acquainted with Buddhism.

This collection is made up of fifteen works of varying length. Most of them are rather short. If we make a selection of the more valuable among them and take them in the order in which they appear in the list of fifteen, we find that the first, the *Short Treatise*, or *Khuddakapatha*, is a brief catechetical presentation of the essentials of Buddhist conduct of life. It is divided into nine brief chapters. Among these we find the formula for declaring oneself a follower of Buddha, the declaration of The Three Refuges. Then there are the Ten Training Precepts, which contain the moral precepts of Buddhism; the Good Omen Discourse, which proclaims in precise detail the fact that the only really good omens of human life are those found in virtuous conduct; The Jewel Discourse, which is a glorious proclamation of the treasure men have in the Buddha, the dharma and the sangha; The Treasure House Discourse, which proclaims the merit, the infinite merit, men obtain by good actions; The Loving-Kindness Discourse, which is an extraordinary statement of Buddhist affection for all the world in its every dimension and for all creatures in it.

The second work of the Short Collection is the *Dhammapada* which may be translated as the Path of Perfection, or the Way of Truth. This must be listed among the greatest spiritual classics of the world. It contains 423 verses in 26 chapters. Each chapter contains a series of reflections on the moral-spiritual life of man, the way of good, and the way of evil, and their consequences. It is a kind of *vade mecum* of all Buddhist monks. Among the most widely read and recited of all Buddhist classics, it has a unique loveliness in the use of metaphor and simile. Most often these are drawn from the natural world; but often, too, they are drawn from the world of man, his cities, his work, his home life.

As a fletcher makes straight his arrow, a wise man makes straight his trembling and unsteady thought, which is difficult to guard, difficult to hold back (33). . . . As a fish taken from his watery home and thrown on the dry ground, our thought trembles all over in order to escape the dominion of Mara, the tempter (34). . . . Like a beautiful flower, full of color and full of scent, are the fine and fruitful words of him who acts accordingly (52). . . . The scent of flowers does not travel against the wind, nor that of sandal wood, or of Tagara and Mallika flowers; but the odour of good people travels even against the wind; a good man pervades every place (54).

Third among these treatises of the Short Collection is the *Udana,* a series of inspired utterances pertaining to the spiritual development of man. These) are given in verse after an introductory section in prose which provides the setting in which the utterance took place.

Fourth among the Short Collection treatises is the *Itivuttakam,* which contains 112 brief Sutras in four series. Each brief Sutra ends with a summary of the teaching in verse form. Some of these are especially fine for the spiritual insight they offer.

The fifth of these treatises in the Short Collection is the *Sutta Nipata,* a more lengthy work and one of the most significant of the early Buddhist texts. It carries the rich emotional, spiritual, and descriptive qualities of the finest Buddhist writings. It has five divisions. The writing is for the most part in verse, although there are generally prose introductions which provide a considerable portion of early Buddhist legendary material. The sections describing the life of the recluse are especially important. They give in depth the entire emotional-spiritual structure of the life of the recluse as lived at this time.

Of the other works among the Short Treatises, two others with special significance are the *Songs of the Elders* and the *Songs of the Nuns.* These have been published together as the *Songs of the Brethren.* As with the works mentioned above, these too carry much of the delicate emotional life of the early Buddhists, a wonderful serenity, a confidence in the doctrine that guided mankind on its way, an elevated spiritual outlook, a friendliness for every living creature, a freshness and enthusiasm for spiritual living.

One final work that might be mentioned as of special significance is the collection of *Jataka,* or *Tales of the Buddha's Previous Lives.* There are 547 of these tales in the *Jataka.* These stories carry much of the mythology of early Buddhism. They also provided a large number of motifs for Buddhist art.

There are a number of other works among the Short Treatises, but these that have been mentioned are especially significant. The others tend to be of rather a late date. All those that have been mentioned are especially valuable for identifying the general mood of early Buddhist development, before the more analytical mood took over. This analytical trend led to the formation of different schools of thought and the production of the classification schemas such as we find in the third section, the *Abhidharma Section.*

3. The third major section of the Hinayana Buddhist scriptures, the *Abhidharma,* has come down to us in two different versions, one in the Theravada Pali canon, the other in the Sarvastivada canon, which was originally in Sanskrit but is now preserved only in Chinese translation. In each case there are seven works in the *Abhidharma Section.* Yet there is no correspondence between the two groups of seven. They agree only in the effort to establish categories

and lists of elements within the Buddhist physical and psychical universe.

Of the seven titles in the *Abhidharma Section* of the Theravada canon the most significant are the *Dhammasangani,* The Listing of Elements; the *Dhatukatha,* Discussion of Elements; and the *Kathavatthu,* The Points of Controversy. This last work is of special importance for identifying the main subjects of discussion between different schools of Buddhist thought.

The seven titles in the *Abhidharma Section* of the Sarvastivada canon are the *Jnana-prasthana,* the Course of Knowledge, by Katyayaniputra; *The Sangiti-paryaya,* Section for Recitation, by Sariputra; *The Prakarana-pada,* by Vasumitra; the *Vijnana-kaya,* Group Concerned with Consciousness, by Devasarman; the *Dhatu-kaya,* Group Concerned with Mental Elements, by Purna; *Dharma-skandha,* Aggregate of Dharmas, by Sariputra; *Prajnapti-sastra,* Text of Instruction, by Maudgalyayana.

All of these works are highly analytical. They seek to classify all reality as this appears in the mind. Thus they are mainly psychological. Although the term *Abhidharma* is etymologically similar to the Western term "metaphysics" there is in reality no real parallel between the content of the Buddhist *Abhidharma* literature and Western metaphysics. Western metaphysics seeks to establish an integral reasoned science of being. There is nothing scientific about the Buddhist *Abhidharma.* It is strictly a classification system in which there is very little reasoned deduction.

Besides these strictly canonical scriptures of Buddhism there are a few works that are considered as paracanonical, works with very great authority in Buddhist tradition but without canonical status in the strict sense of the word. The most important of these works is the *Questions of King Milinda.* Presented in dialogue form, this work is supposedly the account of discussions that took place between the Greek

King Menander and the Buddhist monk, Nagasena. It is sometimes considered to be our earliest extant account of a philosophical discussion between the Oriental and Western worlds.

The *Questions of King Milinda,* sometimes considered the supreme literary masterpiece of Pali literature, is rich in content, concise in presentation, lovely in its imaginative qualities, delicate in its emotional sensitivity. Yet the questions search into the depths of the Buddhist doctrine of reality. Of special significance are the questions concerning the Buddhist denial of a self or a personality, the Nirvana experience, the transmigration process, and the earthly and transearthly aspect of Buddha. The answers given are not always reasoned answers, nor are they completely satisfying to our Western philosophical mentality. The questions are solved too frequently by adroit use of analogy and comparison, without the hard metaphysical insight sought by Western philosophers. Yet the essential insights into Buddhist doctrine are there, with a clarity and fullness difficult to find anywhere else in the entire collection of Buddhist writings of the Hinayana schools. Recognized by Buddhist writers as having exceptionally high authority, this work has been much quoted from a very early period.

Besides the basic scriptures of Buddhism and these paracanonical works, the great mass of Buddhist writings is composed of commentaries on the scriptures and of special studies. The greatest master of Theravada thought, Buddhaghosa, wrote an amazing amount of commentary on the books of Pali canon. He also composed the single great synthesis of Theravada Buddhism, the *Visuddhimagga, The Path of Purity.* The name Buddhaghosa, which means the voice of Buddha, is renowned throughout the Hinayana Buddhist world of southeast Asia. His writings were preserved both in Ceylon and in Burma, whence they were communicated to Thailand and Cambodia.

After Buddhaghosa, two other writers of some renown

are mentioned in the Hinayana Pali tradition, Buddhadatta and Dhammapala. Both of these came from southern India and did their work in Ceylon. Since their work is substantially in the tradition established by Buddhaghosa we can conclude that they also studied and worked in Ceylon. Indeed it was here in Ceylon that the Buddhist Pali canon was preserved until our own times, for strangely enough no substantial amount of Buddhist writing, either in Pali or in Sanskrit, was preserved in India.

PART II

THE NEW BUDDHISM

CHAPTER IX

THE GREAT
TRANSFORMATION

During the last two centuries of the pre-Christian era a profound change was taking place within Buddhism, the deepest, most significant change that was to appear in this tradition. It divided Buddhism permanently into the Buddhism of
the Great Vehicle and Buddhism of the Lesser Vehicle—re-
spectively, Mahayana and Hinayana Buddhism.

Mahayana Buddhism might be called a neo-Buddhism in
contrast to the older Hinayana Buddhism. But even while
calling one older and the other newer it must be kept in
mind that the older Buddhism has continued vigorously up
to the present and that the roots of the newer Buddhism
reach back to the time of Buddha himself.

A proper understanding of the relationship between the
Mahayana and Hinayana Buddhism has been most difficult
for Western scholars, although an understanding of this relationship remains most important not only for the scholar
but for anyone who would do even a limited amount of reading in any of the Buddhist writings.

Some scholars, such as Stcherbatsky, consider that the
new, religiously oriented Buddhism has very little in common with the older areligious ascetic discipline of Hinayana
Buddhism. Indeed on first sight the new Buddhism does
seem to contradict the most elementary principles on which
the earlier Buddhism was founded. Everything is changed—
the spiritual and moral ideals, imagination and emotions, the

metaphysics, the process of salvation, the entire structuring of human life.

Religiously there is in the Mahayana a divinized Buddha, a new heavenly court of saints and semidivine beings with magical powers to aid and guide man in his search for liberation. There are shrines and images, invocations and prayer formulas, festivals, colourful processions, songs of exaltation, experience of divine presence, pictures of paradise, legends of the glorious deeds of the divine appearances on earth, miracles of every kind. Even the physical world was profoundly altered by the divine presence when Buddha was on earth.

This new sense of the divine and the miraculous can be seen in the following passage which describes the response of earth to the Buddha presence:

> As he came into the city, the depressions in the ground rose up so that the whole surface was on the same level. All unsightly rocks, gravel, and pebbles disappeared into the earth, leaving it covered with masses of flowers. Flowering trees blossomed; fruit-bearing trees bore fruit. The ponds in which lotuses had been sown, pools full of cool water on the right and on the left of the roadway, became covered with fragrant blue, white and red lotuses. . . . The blind saw; the deaf heard. The insane recovered their reason; the sick were healed, and women with child were safely delivered. The naked appeared clad, and the fetters of those in bondage were loosened. Jewels rattled in their caskets and earthenware vessels clattered. All the seven-stringed lutes in the city, all the Indian lutes, all the mandolins, flutes, tambours, drums and cymbals, without any cause, without being touched, gave forth music. Parrots, sarikas, crows, swans, and peacocks all uttered their notes.
>
> The Buddha walked without touching the ground for even as much as the width of four fingers, and yet the impress of the wheel-marks on his feet, complete with a thousand spokes, hub, and every part, was visible on the ground. In the sky devas played on thousands of celestial musical instruments and rained down celestial flowers" (*Mahavastu* i, 308).

The earlier Buddhism now gave way before an emotional life based on devotion to the Buddha as a merciful divine being, an imaginative life that produced art and ritual of a very advanced and lofty sort. It also produced a highly imaginative literature such as we find in *Buddhacarita*. Intellectually the earlier Hinayana scholasticism now gave way before a new and exalted intuitional mysticism. Stated briefly we can say that the Mahayana represents both an emotional and an intellectual deepening of the Buddhist experience.

Three major forces were at work producing this change, forces within Buddhism, new developments in the surrounding Hindu tradition, and influences from Hellenism brought into India at the time of Alexander.

Within Buddhism extensive changes had taken place. There was an extensive popularization of Buddhism. The very success that Buddhism had under Asoka in the third century B.C. and in the following centuries established new pressures unknown to Buddhism during its first period when it was under the strong spiritual controls of the wandering recluses and the monks settled in their monasteries. The position of the Arhat elite was now challenged. A certain weight of lay religion was felt. New emotions were stirring in a people not at all attracted by a legalistic discipline or doctrinal scholasticism. These latter were drying up the inner spiritual-emotional forces of the earlier Buddhism.

A similar situation was developing at this time in the surrounding Hindu tradition. The old pastoral-ritual religion of the early Aryan period and the later Brahmanic intuitional religion of the upper classes had never supplied the religious needs of the people. The older forms of Hinduism were giving way to the devotional theistic religion expressed in the *Bhagavadgita*. This devotional movement would produce a new set of Hindu scriptures, the Puranas, during the next ten centuries. These would henceforth provide the basic structure of popular Hinduism as it has existed ever since. This new Hinduism with its temples and image worship, its salvation by grace of a benign deity, its mythology, its emotional intensity, its love relation between the divine and the human realms of reality, all of these developments had an influence on the Buddhism of the period.

Also in the background of Indian spiritual development we find a strong influence from Hellenism with its pantheon of deities and its anthropomorphic ways of dealing with the gods. Especially in the making of sacred images this influence was manifesting itself in India at this time.

But even while we outline the changes taking place to produce a neo-Buddhism, and while we study the discontinuity between the older and the newer forms of Buddhism, we must keep in mind that there was a profound continuity within Buddhist development. This continuity has come to be better understood and accepted by recent scholars. To some extent the earlier emphasis on discontinuity resulted from the fact that Western scholarship first discovered the earlier Hinayana Buddhism and its scriptures. The Hinayana became identified with authentic Buddhism. Then as Western scholarship discovered the Mahayana texts, the differences appeared so great that Mahayana was considered a Western-influenced unauthentic type of Buddhism that had relatively little relationship with the true Hinayana Buddhism.

Yet, as Western study proceeded, it became clear that the main elements in Mahayana Buddhism were present in Buddhist tradition from the beginning. There were even indications that the distinctive Mahayana ideas had as much foundation in the original tradition as the opposed Hinayana ideas. It is now clear that Mahayana Buddhism was not derived from the Hinayana but was a distinctive tradition from the earliest times. Its full expression required, however, a longer period of preparation.

The greatest source of difficulty in understanding the unity of the Buddhist tradition may be simply that the inner richness of Buddhist development is such that it excessively burdens our minds when we try to understand it. The inner tensions and apparent contradictions are a strain on the mind.

It is easy to escape these tensions and the burden of integration if we merely say that they are two different things. It is more difficult but more true to the reality to see these differences and apparent contradictions as creative tensions that have given great vitality and inexhaustible richness to a single spiritual and intellectual tradition.

While the two go back in origin to the early Buddhism, it is true also that the Mahayana in its full expression did develop later. It had a late flowering. Mahayana also conceived itself from the beginning as opposed to many of the basic doctrines of the Hinayana tradition. The earliest Mahayana literature, especially the *Lotus Sutra,* is very precise on this point. Indeed we date the very existence of the Mahayana from the time when the upholders of the Mahayana Buddhism claimed to possess the only way of salvation in opposition to the Hinayana. The followers of Mahayana even invented the name "Mahayana," the broad or great way of salvation for all men, and the name "Hinayana," the way of salvation mainly for those who went forth into the life of the recluse. Then they appropriated the grander title for the newer tradition while bestowing the lesser title on the Buddhism of the earlier period.

But however we resolve these issues of the continuity and discontinuity of Mahayana and Hinayana Buddhism, the Mahayana tradition as we know it came to its first full expression in the opening centuries of the Christian period after some centuries of development prior to this time. Within this new tradition, the fundamental Buddhist doctrines of Buddha, dharma, and sangha have all been transformed. The significance of the Four Noble Truths and the Eightfold Path is also changed. Every aspect of Buddhism is newly structured according to expanded principles. Even the sense of personal identity of the follower of Buddha is altered. From being a lowly creature, the follower of dharma now feels that he himself has a Buddha nature. All reality is lifted up to participate in the eternal transearthly existence of the Buddha.

CHAPTER X

THE ETERNAL BUDDHA

The most significant development in the neo-Buddhism of the Mahayana tradition was the new doctrine that Buddha, in his true reality, was a transearthly, eternal being who appears on earth periodically on a salvation mission to suffering mankind. This change is of central importance because the person of Buddha looms massively over the entire history of Buddhist development. Buddha is much more central to Buddhism than Mohammed is to Islam, than Confucius is to Confucianism, or Lao Tzu to Taoism. Questions concerning Buddha formed the main point of discussion during the most crucial period of Buddhist thought development, the period that lasted from the time of Asoka until the beginning of the Christian period.

There is a certain feeling in the earlier scriptures that the followers of Buddha really knew who Buddha was. But as time passed they found that they could not really cope with the Buddha reality, at least not as well as they thought. This being was more mysterious in his person, in his mission to mankind, in his work as teacher and guide, than men had thus far realized. Deep within the Indian soul was the sense of the divine manifesting itself in reality, both human and cosmic. In a Upanishadic text speaking of Brahman, we read: "You are woman, you are man, you are youth and maiden. An old man you totter with a staff. Being born, you face in every direction. You are the dark-blue bee, the green parrot with red eyes. You are the thundercloud with lightning in its womb. You are the seasons and the seas. Without beginning, you abide immanent in things, you from whom all beings are born" (*Svetesvatara Upanishad,* iv, 3–4). It is not surprising then that a spiritual teacher so impressive as Buddha should gradually be seen as a manifestation of some transearthly reality.

This exaltation took some time to achieve, but it was clearly attained in the *Mahavastu,* a work that is especially significant as providing the first extensive statement of the transearthly character of Buddha. The conclusion in the *Mahavastu* is that "There is nothing in the Buddhas that can be measured by the standard of the world, but everything relating to the great seers is transearthly. Likewise the experience of the Buddhas is transearthly" (i, 159). The *Mahavastu* constantly objects to those who do not appreciate the higher qualities of the Buddha. "They teach that Buddhas are of the world" (i, 96). The full statement of the doctrine was, however, not attained until the composition of the *Lotus Sutra.* "The Tathagata who so long ago was perfectly enlightened is unlimited in the duration of his life, he is everlasting" (*Lotus Sutra,* 302).

But immediately when Buddha begins to be exalted to transearthly status the problem occurs as regards the earthly presence of Buddha: Is this reality or only appearance? The problem of the followers of Buddha was similar to the problem of the Indian people generally. It was the problem, not of eternal reality, but of temporal reality. The divine aspect of Buddha, that was not difficult to explain. The human aspect of Buddha, that was difficult to explain. How account for Buddha's earthly presence and the deeds performed by him here in the world of time and space? If "there is nothing in the Buddhas that can be measured by the standard of the world," then how explain the visible presence of Buddha manifested here in the world?

This problem occurs in many of the later writings even of Theravada Buddhism. It occurs both in the *Points of Controversy* and in the *Questions of King Milinda.* In the *Points of Controversy,* one proposition states: "It is not correct to say 'The Exalted Buddha lived in the world of mankind.' " This proposition is based on a quotation from the Psalms of the Nuns, that "The Buddha born in the world, grew up in the world, dwelt having overcome the world, undefiled by the world." That Buddha was undefiled by the world led some to conclude that Buddha was never really in the world.

The answer given by the Theravada defender is in the form of a question that surveys the whole life of Buddha in terms of historic time, earthly space and human activity. "But are there not shrines, parks, settlements, towns, kingdoms, countries mentioned by the Buddha? And was he not born at Lumbini, enlightened under the Bodhi tree? Was not the Dharma-wheel set rolling by him at Benares? Did he not renounce the will to live at the Chapala shrine? Did he not complete existence at Kusinara?" (*Katha.* xviii, 1.)

While the *Mahavastu* grants all this, it insists that even in the physical actions of Buddha there is no equation with the actions of men as generally known to us. The eyesight of Buddha cannot even be measured by ordinary norms. "Yet this physical eye of the Buddhas has the same colour, the same mode of working and the same position in the body as it has in other beings" (i, 159).

Was Buddha ever born as other men are born? The answer given is that Buddha only appears to have a father and a mother. His corporeal existence is not due to any sexual union of parents, for this would in some manner require a real earthly form. "Although the Blessed One's corporeal existence is not due to the sexual union of any parents, yet the Buddhas can point to their fathers and mothers. This is mere conformity with the world" (*Mahavastu* i, 170).

What then of the emotional life of Buddha? If indeed he never experienced sorrow, how could he feel true compassion? How could there be any real interpersonal communion with Buddha, such as had existed throughout the centuries of Buddhist history? Theravada Buddhists felt this point rather

keenly. Some Buddhists, however, were willing to deny the
existence of any emotional life in Buddha in order to main-
tain his exalted status. Thus one group proposed: "The
Exalted Buddha felt no pity." This was too much for the
Theravadins, who responded: "But this implies that neither
did he feel love nor sympathetic joy nor equanimity. You
deny. But could he have these and yet lack pity? Your proposition implies also that he was ruthless" (*Katha.* xvii, 3).

So also the Buddha is considered free from passion. "From
Dipankara onwards, the Tathagata is always free from
passion. That the Buddha has a son, Rahula, to show, is mere
conformity with the world" (*Mahavastu* i, 170). This attitude
towards Buddha is carried out to such extravagant expression
that "The conduct of the Exalted One is transearthly, his
root of virtue is transcendental. The Seer's walking, standing, sitting, and lying down are transcendental" (*Mahavastu*
i, 167, 168). Of the Buddhas, "It is true that they wash their
feet, but no dust ever adheres to them; their feet remain
clear as lotus-leaves. This washing is mere conformity with
the world. . . . It is true that the Buddhas bathe, but no
dirt is found on them; their bodies are radiant like the golden
amaranth. Their bathing is mere conformity with the world"
(*Mahavastu* i, 168).

The most important effort to deal with this problem of
the eternal and the temporal existence of Buddha is found
in the Mahayana doctrine of the Threefold Body of Buddha.
Buddha is considered to have an essential, an eternal body
that is called his Dharma Body. This, in the final analysis is
the only real body possessed by Buddha. There is another
body, his Transformation Body. In this body, he is born on
earth, he teaches dharma, he brings about the salvation of
mankind, and then passes into Nirvana. This is the body of
the historical Buddha. The third body of Buddha, the Body
of Bliss, is the glorified body in which Buddha manifests himself with radiant splendour to the assemblies of the Bodhisattvas. It is shown only in special circumstances.

The doctrine of the three bodies later became an integral part of Buddhist metaphysics. It is developed with special clarity in the *Awakening of Faith in the Mahayana,* attributed to Ashvaghosa. By this concept of a Threefold Body, the entire problem of the relation between the phenomenal and transphenomenal worlds is discussed in depth. The eternal body of Buddha eventually came to be considered as the true body of all living beings, the *urgrund* of the universal order of things. Through this discussion of the Threefold Body of Buddha we emerge into the problem of our deepest human identity. There is basic similarity between this doctrine and the Brahman-Atman doctrine of the Upanishadic writings of Brahmanism.

CHAPTER XI

THE NEW WAY
OF PERFECTION

In Mahayana Buddhism the highest message of Buddha to mankind is: "Forsake all doubt and uncertainty; you shall become Buddhas. Rejoice!" (*Lotus Sutra* ii, 144.)

Once phenomenal reality is seen as a manifestation of some transearthly reality, then the deepest identity of man is found not directly in himself but in the eternal reality. Man's partial being has no significance except by its self-realization in absolute being. Within the Buddhist context, the true realization of man is found in his attainment of Buddhahood, for the Buddha reality is eventually the reality of all living beings. This doctrine was not fully worked out in the minds of Buddhist authors themselves until later on in Buddhist development, especially in Chinese Buddhism. But from the beginning of the Mahayana the ideal was there. As Buddha in his Transformation Body attained the status of a fully illumined Buddha, so he has shown all mankind the way to attain this same status.

All men have this same capacity. This is known as the Bodhisattva doctrine, the doctrine that everyone is called to realize his proper nature as a Buddha-being. This establishes the foundation of a new spiritual discipline. The way of perfection is no longer the career of the Arhat seeking Nirvana; it is the career of the Bodhisattva seeking Buddhahood.

There is some precedent for this ideal in the Theravada

tradition. There, however, the Bodhisattva ideal is applied only to Buddha during his period of search for enlightenment. Yet the explanation given is such that the Bodhisattva ideal seems to be an ideal possible to others. It did not at first exclude or take the place of the Arhat ideal of the earlier Buddhism. In the Sarvastivada tradition the Bodhisattva ideal is applied to everyone. Frequent mention is made of three ideals of spiritual perfection that came to be known as the three vehicles or the three careers. There was first the career of the Arhat, the disciple of Buddha. Then there was the career of the Pratyekabuddha. This ideal was never fully developed. It indicated someone who entered on the way of perfection with a certain independence and for himself alone. This ideal was too asocial to be satisfying generally. Then there was the third career, that of the Bodhisattva, the career of one who sought illumination and the final status of Buddhahood both for himself and for all mankind.

Gradually this third ideal came to dominate all the ideals in the Mahayana schools of Buddhism. The final stage in establishing the Mahayana tradition was reached when this ideal of the Bodhisattva became not only the most worthy ideal of Buddhism, but the only true ideal, the only way of perfection, the only way in which anyone attains liberation. If Buddha, during his earthly life, did not teach this ideal, but rather that of the Arhat, the reason was that men could not at first understand or aspire to a career so sublime. They had first to be attracted to the lesser ideal of the Arhat. Then at a later period, when the minds of men had developed sufficiently, the nobler ideal could be presented to them.

As with the ideal of the Arhat, so with the ideal of Nirvana. Buddha, during his earthly life, did not speak of Buddhahood; he spoke of Nirvana as the final bliss to be sought. Of men generally, Buddha said:

> They are hard to correct, proud, hypocritical, crooked, malignant, ignorant, dull; hence they do not hear the good Buddha-call, not once in ten thousand births. To those, son

of Sari, I show a device and say: "Put an end to your trouble. When I perceive creatures vexed with mishap I make them see Nirvana. So I reveal all the laws that are ever holy and correct from the very first. The son of Buddha who has completed his course shall become a Leader. It is simply my skilfulness that prompts me to manifest the three vehicles; for in reality there is but one vehicle and one track; there is also only one instruction by the leaders" (*Lotus Sutra* ii, 65–68).

This expedient use of the Nirvana concept is also indicated in the passage:

> I show Nirvana to the ignorant with low dispositions, who have followed no course of duty under many thousands of Buddhas, who are bound to continued existence and are wretched (*Lotus* ii, 45). . . . But there are others so gifted and so disciplined that I am able to announce to them: "In future you shall become Buddhas benevolent and compassionate." Hearing this, all of them are pervaded with delight. We shall become Buddhas pre-eminent in the world. And I, seeing their conduct, will again reveal expanded Sutras (*Lotus* ii, 50–51).

While this seems a perfectly legitimate procedure, this teaching of the ignorant by using language they can understand and to which they can respond, it posed a delicate moral question to the early exponents of the Mahayana, especially to the author of the *Lotus Sutra*. In this Sutra the first clear effort was made to disengage the Mahayana completely from the Hinayana tradition. But even while the disengagement was taking place there was a need to justify this earlier phase of Buddhist teaching. If Buddha taught and acted in accord with the Hinayana tradition, a certain deception seemed to be involved. Thus with the apparent extinction of the Buddha at the time of his death and entry into Nirvana—why was this done, if in truth Buddha was an eternal being with eternal existence and totally beyond extinction? The explanation given is: "The Tathagata who so long ago was perfectly enlightened is unlimited in the duration of his life, he is everlasting. Without becoming extinct, the Tathagata makes a show of extinction on behalf of those who have to be educated" (*Lotus* xv). Education then is the motive. Awareness of the ambiguity is so vivid to the writer, however, that he must state over and over again: "Such, young men of good family, is the Tathagata's manner of teaching; when the Tathagata speaks in this way, there is on his part no falsehood (*Lotus* xv).

Still not satisfied, the author tells a parable about a physician whose sons became ill from drinking poison. The physician prepared an antidote for the poison. Some of the sons took the remedy and were cured. Others were so crazed by the poison that they would not take the medicine prepared for them.

> Then the physician reflects thus: These sons of mine must have become perverted in their notions owing to this poison or venom, as they do not take the remedy nor hail me. Therefore I will by an effective device induce these sons to take this remedy. Prompted by this desire he speaks to those sons as follows: "I am old, young men of good family, decrepit, advanced in years, and my term of life is near at hand; but be not sorry, young men of good family, do not feel dejected; here I have prepared a great remedy for you; if you want it, you may take it." Having thus admonished them, he skilfully betakes himself to another part of the country and lets his sick sons know that he has departed life. They are extremely sorry and bewail him extremely: "So then he is dead, our father and protector; he who begat us; he, so full of bounty! Now we are left without a protector." Fully aware of their being orphans and of having no refuge, they are continually plunged in sorrow, by which their perverted notions make room for right notions. They acknowledged that the remedy possessed the right colour, smell, and taste, so that they instantly take it, and by taking it are delivered from their evil. Then, on knowing that these sons are delivered from evil, the physician shows himself again. "Now, young men of good family, what is your opinion? Would

anyone charge that physician with falsehood on account of his using that device?" "No, certainly not, Lord; certainly not, Blessed One." "In the same manner, young men of good family, I have arrived at supreme, perfect enlightenment since an immense, incalculable number of a hundred thousand of aeons, but from time to time I display such able devices to creatures, with the view of educating them, without there being in that respect any falsehood on my part" (*Lotus* xv).

Thus the masters of the early Mahayana, in order to place the new vision in its proper context, evolved an explanation based on the historical evolution of Buddhist doctrine. The real truth had to emerge in historical sequence. Mankind needed a period of pedagogical preparation.

Both a new type of teaching and a new type of understanding had to be developed for communication to man of that vision of reality which alone would provide a final goal for man. This final truth of things is so sublime that men will never have adequate understanding of it. In this we see the intense search for the highest spiritual goals that characterized the mental life of India. Seldom have men reached for higher goals. Seldom has such awareness been shown by man of the tender concern for man on the part of higher powers; the highest reality sought to lift up earthly reality to share its own form of existence. Thus Buddha is presented as saying: "I would be guilty of envy, should I, after reaching the spotless eminent state of enlightenment, establish anyone in the inferior path. That would not befit me. There is no envy whatever in me; no jealousy, no desire, nor passion. Therefore I am the Buddha, because the world follows my teaching" (*Lotus* ii, 56–57).

So with Buddha's teaching, he is leading men to a goal far beyond Nirvana, although men do not realize it.

It is, O Lord, as if some man having come to a friend's house got drunk or fell asleep, and that friend bound a priceless gem within his garment, with the thought: Let this gem be his. After a while, O Lord, that man rises from his seat and travels further; he goes to some other country, where he meets incessant difficulties, and has great trouble to find food and clothing. By dint of great exertion he is hardly able to obtain a bit of food, with which [however] he is contented and satisfied. The old friend of that man, O Lord, who bound within the man's garment that priceless gem, happens to see him again and says: How is it, good friend, that you have such difficulty in seeking food and clothing, while I, in order that you should live in ease, good friend, have bound within your garment a priceless gem, quite sufficient to fulfil all your wishes? I have given you that gem, my good friend; the very gem I have bound within your garment. Still you are deliberating: What has been bound? by whom? for what reason and purpose? It is something foolish, my good friend, to be contented, when you must with such difficulty procure food and clothing. Go, my good friend, betake yourself, with this gem, to some great city, exchange the gem for money, and with that money do all that can be done with money.

In the same manner, O Lord, has the Tathagata formerly, when he still followed the course of duty of a Bodhisattva, raised in us also ideas of omniscience, but we, O Lord, did not perceive nor know it. We fancied, O Lord, that on the stage of Arhat we had reached Nirvana. We live in difficulty, O Lord, because we content ourselves with such a trifling degree of knowledge (*Lotus* viii, 33). . . . We were living in this world, O Lord, with dull understanding and in ignorance, under the mastership of the Blessed One; for we were contented with a little of Nirvana; we required nothing higher, nor even cared for it. But the Friend of the world has taught us better: This is no blessed Rest at all; the full knowledge of the highest persons, that is blessed Rest, that is supreme beatitude (*Lotus* viii, 43–44).

In further explanation of the higher and lower realms of reality and of knowledge, the Mahayana developed the theory of the twofold truth, apparent truth and real truth, which is also described as relative truth and absolute truth: *samvritti-*

satya and *paramartha-satya*. Absolute truth alone is real in any final sense. Yet man is such that he must pass through a period when he perceives only relative truth. Buddha also, if he is to communicate with mankind, must enter into the realm of relative truth.

CHAPTER XII

REDEMPTIVE SUFFERING

One of the most impressive aspects of Mahayana Buddhism is the transformation it produced in the attitude toward sorrow. Hinayana Buddhism dealt with sorrow as a thing to be surmounted on an individual basis. A stifling thing, sorrow was the supreme evil. Each individual person must master and triumph over it. The laws of moral determination assigned to each individual the responsibility for his condition. He alone had the power to perform the good deeds that would bring relief from his human miseries.

In Mahayana Buddhism one individual could assist others, could bear the sorrow of others, could bestow his own merit upon others. The new ideal was to become a Buddha-being, to accomplish a universal mission such as Buddha accomplished. This involved a concern for others similar to the concern Buddha manifested when, after his enlightenment, he chose a career of assistance to the manyfolk rather than a career of solitary wandering or of quiet retreat from human habitation. This mission of Buddha involved the burdensome tasks of travel, teaching, weariness, disappointment, and a general entering into the human turmoil. The early Sutras insist on the deliberate, well-considered choice made by Buddha of this active, suffering life.

Yet the aid bestowed by Buddha is described in the earlier Hinayana writings as a thing primarily of instruction in the nature of the human condition and how to attain relief by following the Eightfold Path. It is only in the *Jataka* tales that we find Buddha presented as one suffering directly for others. There Buddha offers himself, all his possessions, even his own life, for the welfare of others. In the story of the starving tigress and her cubs Buddha gives himself to be their food. Many other such stories are recounted in the *Jataka* tales about the virtuous deeds of the great Bodhisattva in his many prior appearances on earth. By these deeds he gradually accumulated the merit to become the Buddha known to us in this particular aeon of time. But even in the *Jataka* tales we do not find a real transfer of merit or a vicarious suffering in the more strict meaning of the term.

The most important Hinayana source for the suffering-saviour ideal of later Mahayana development is found in the doctrine of the stages of mental concentration. After the first meditations on the insubstantial and repulsive aspects of life and before entering on the more abstract stages of intellectual insight there is a stage of spiritual progress designated as the attainment of boundless freedom of mind, *cetovimutti*. This boundless freedom results from the breaking of the barriers between the individual and all other living beings. The new relationship with the universal order of things, described in terms of emotional relationships, represents the highest fruition of the emotional life of Buddhism. After this stage the spiritual life of Buddhism tends towards the higher intellectual abstractions in which these emotional experiences play a much smaller part.

In this stage of boundless freedom of mind a person attains an experience of the four Divine Abodes, the *Brahma-Vihara*. These are the states of loving-friendship, compassion, delight in the joy of others, and equanimity. All of these involve a going-forth from the confinement of a person's own emotional life to a sharing in the lives of others. The first relationship established is the love relationship of *metta*. The next two follow logically from the first, for any love relationship has a sympathetic feeling for the afflictions endured by others and a delight in the well-being of others. The final aspect of a truly sound love relationship must be a certain detachment that enables a person to avoid emotional upset that might arise from this association.

This Buddhist relationship with others must include all living beings. It must be universal, completely unrestricted. If any single being is excluded from sharing in this relationship, then it is not soundly established. The ideal sought by the person practising these virtues is to pervade the entire world with this vast feeling of oneness with and concern for others. According to Buddhaghosa the thought of the well-being of others must be projected to the different quarters of the universe. "May all beings in the eastern direction be free from enmity, affliction and anxiety, and live happily. May all beings in the western, northern, southern directions, may all beings in the downward direction, the upward direction, may all be free from enmity, affliction and anxiety, and live happily" (*Vis.* ix, 52). This is done first with loving-friendship, then with compassion, sympathetic joy, and equanimity, so that no being is excluded from entering into this intercommunion of love, goodness and well-being.

In attaining this loving relationship with others there is a primary insistence on overcoming all feelings of resentment towards others, no matter what afflictions we sustain from them. "Hatred is not cured by hatred" (*Dh.* 5). Buddhaghosa tells many instances in the life of Buddha when he endured affliction from others without feeling any antipathies, but only love towards the person. He also quotes the instruction of Buddha: "Monks, even though bandits were to sever you limb from limb with a two-handled saw, whoever would entertain hate within his own breast for that reason would not be carrying out my instruction" (*Maj.* i, 129; *Vis.* ix, 15). Only when resentment is fully overcome will a person be able to project a loving-kindness to all the world of living beings.

But if loving-friendship and nonresentment are the social virtues best understood and most practised by the early Buddhists, there was a progressive emphasis on compassion by the later Buddhists. The early Buddhists were still self-orientated in their life attitude. The highest virtues were looked upon mainly as stages of inner purification of a person's own self. This residual self-concern remains until the later development of the Sarvastivada teaching. There is no convincing indication that in the Theravada teaching there was any real communication of merit to another. Each must gain his own merit according to the laws of karma. This law of karma was so fundamental to the entire Indian tradition that it is surprising to find how extensively it was surmounted by the later Buddhist doctrines of vicarious suffering and of the communication of merit to others.

If we compare the *Abhidharmakosa* of Vasubandhu with the *Visuddhimagga* of Buddhaghosa we find that the Sarvastivadins had gone further than the Theravadins in this direction. In the ninth chapter of Buddhaghosa where he is concerned with this subject we find no mention of suffering for others or of transferring merit to others. In the *Abhidharmakosa* there is still no question of bestowing merit upon others, but there is a willingness expressed to suffer to attain the welfare of others. When the question arises concerning why the Bodhisattvas undertake such extensive burdens the answer given by Vasubandhu is that they seek the welfare of others and wish "to bring them out of the great sea of suffering in which they are immersed." Utterly detached from their own selves they are ready "to endure countless pains in their concern for others" (*Abhidharmakosa* ii, 192).

In the Mahayana tradition, as this developed in the *Lotus Sutra,* the sense of compassion, of *karuna,* is very strong, but there is still no question of the Bodhisattva suffering the pains of others or of transferring merit to others. This is a preaching, illuminating Sutra that offers a way of salvation by devotion to Buddha. This leads eventually to sharing the divine existence of Buddhahood. An infinite amount of merit is gained by the simplest act of devotion, so that no real transfer of merit and no vicarious suffering are needed.

The earliest appearance of a fully developed doctrine of

vicarious suffering is found in the *Wisdom Sutras*. The purpose of suffering is to assist others as well as oneself to attain the perfect illumination in which salvation consists. "Subhuti: What is the manifestation of the great compassion? The Lord: That the Bodhisattva, the great being, who courses on the Bodhisattva-pilgrimage, thinks that 'for the sake of the weal of every single being will I, dwelling in the hells for aeons countless like the sands of the Ganges, experience therein the cuttings up, the breakings up, the poundings, the torments, the roastings, until that being has become established in the Buddha-cognition. This excessive fortitude, this indefatigability, for the sake of all beings, that is called the manifestation of the great compassion' " (Conze, *Wisdom Selections*, p. 41). The saying is repeated many times that the Bodhisattva will endure endless pains for endless periods of time until every single being is brought to Nirvana.

Associated with this doctrine of vicarious suffering is the doctrine of the transfer of merit. The doctrine of the accumulation of merit is found in Buddhist teaching from the beginning. One of the main quests of the individual in early Buddhism was the storing up of a mass of merit that would assure the well-being of the person in the future phases of his existence until he attained final liberation in Nirvana. Merit was gained principally by giving alms, especially alms to the Buddhist monastic establishments, but also by following the basic rules of sound moral conduct and by the practise of the Buddhist meditative discipline.

There was in this early period no question of communication of merit. This was not fully developed until much later. The doctrine of the transfer of merit found its supreme expression in the teachings of Santi Deva in the seventh century A.D. One of his finest passages speaks of the application of his merits to others:

> May all that are sick of body and soul in every region find oceans of bliss and delight through my merits. Whilst embodied life lasts on, may they never lack happiness, and

forever may the world win the joy of the Sons of Enlightenment. . . . As long as the heavens and the earth abide, may
I continue to overcome the world's sorrows. May all the
world's suffering be cast upon me, and may the world be
made happy by all the merits of the Bodhisattva (Barnett,
tr., *Path of Light,* pp. 24–26).

He constantly repeated that it was certainly better that
he alone should be afflicted than that all other beings should
endure endless sorrow. His final motive was that "all may be
full of love for one another" (Barnett, p. 59).

In this later saint of Buddhism one of the most profound
trends within the entire tradition came to its final fruition.
It was the desire not only to experience but in some manner
to become identical with the entire order of things, to be
immersed in the highest experience possible of the total
order of things even though this was eventually a world of
sunyata, of emptiness. Indeed it was precisely in this final
mystery of things, this emptiness that is somehow a fullness,
that Santi Deva found his final life experience:

> I will cease to live as self, and will take as myself my fel-
> low-creatures. We love our hands and other limbs, as mem-
> bers of the body; then why not love other living beings, as
> members of the universe? . . . Make thyself a spy for the
> service of others, and whatsoever thou seest in thy body's
> work that is good for thy fellows, perform it so that it may
> be conveyed to them (Barnett, p. 80).

Santi Deva looked forward to the supreme peace to be
attained by all through his endurance of pain:

> Then when will the day come when I may bring peace
> to them that are tortured in the fire of sorrow by my min-
> istrations of sweetness born from the rain-clouds of my
> righteousness, and when may I reverently declare to the souls
> who imagine a real world that all is void and righteousness is
> gathered by looking beyond the Veiled Truth? (Barnett, p.
> 84.)

CHAPTER XIII

THE RELIGIOUS VIRTUES

The new situation called forth new virtues with a religious
rather than a moral emphasis. Faith, worship, devotion,
merit, grace: these provide the context in which Buddhism
lived during this period. All of these tended towards the
perfect wisdom of Buddhahood as a final goal. For the
greater number of the people, however, this higher wisdom
could not be expected immediately. Their best hope for
salvation lay in the intensity of their faith and devotion.
This in turn would bring down a heavenly grace that would
lead them on to a higher stage of life and enable them finally
to attain the highest form of enlightenment.

These religious virtues have their first full expression in
the *Lotus Sutra,* one of the earliest of the Mahayana scriptures. In this Sutra, Buddha reveals the higher truth of Buddhahood as the goal to which all men are called. This revelation requires a new type of faith on the part of the disciple.

It is only on the assurance that his teaching will be accepted by faith that Buddha presents his revelation. Three
times Sariputra asked: "Let the Lord explain, let the Blessed
One expound this matter, for in this assembly, O Lord, there
are many hundreds, many thousands, many hundred thousands of living beings who have seen former Buddhas, who
are intelligent, and will believe, value and accept the words
of the Lord" (*Lotus* ii, 31). After the third repetition of this
request the response was given: "Now that you entreat the

Tathagata a third time, Sariputra, I will answer you. Listen, then, Sariputra, take well and duly to heart what I am saying; I am going to speak" (*Lotus* ii, 36).

At this moment not everyone was willing to listen with humble attention: "Now it happened that five thousand proud monks, nuns, and lay devotees of both sexes in the congregation rose from their seats and, after saluting with their heads the Lord's feet, went to leave the assembly" (*Lotus* ii, 36).

Only after this solemn preparation was the revelation given:

> By means of one sole vehicle, that is the Buddha-vehicle, Sariputra, do I teach creatures the law; there is no second vehicle, nor a third. , . . In respect to these things believe my words, Sariputra, value them, take them to heart; for there is no falsehood in the Tathagatas, Sariputra. There is but one vehicle, Sariputra, and that the Buddha-vehicle (*Lotus,* ii 36). . . . Therefore try to understand the mystery of the Buddhas, the holy masters of the world, forsake all doubt and uncertainty: you shall become Buddhas; rejoice! (*Lotus* ii, 144).

If the new objective in the Mahayana is the attainment of Buddahood, this sublime destiny requires a new type of faith far superior to that of the earlier Buddhism which sought only Nirvana. This faith does, however, have some continuity with the faith in the earlier Buddhism. Hinayana, too, had been founded on attachment to Buddha: "Because dharma has been well taught by me, made manifest, opened up, made known, stripped of its swathings, all those who have enough faith in me, enough affection, are bound for heaven" (*Maj.* i, 142).

Yet a Nirvana or a heavenly destiny was more easily comprehended than the dharma of Buddhahood. "It is not by reasoning, Sariputra, that the dharma is to be found; it is beyond the pale of reasoning, and must be learned from

the Tathagata" (*Lotus* ii, 36). Faith now becomes so powerful that the merit obtained by the practise of all the other
virtues during eight hundred thousand aeons of time "does
not equal one thousandth of the merit obtained by a single
act of faith" (*Lotus* xvi, 16).

Associated with faith in the new Buddhism is the new
development of worship. Buddha himself had taught a strictly
human discipline as the way of salvation. His last words
were, "Work out your salvation with diligence" (*D.* ii, 156).
In his discourses we find no reference to higher powers, no
prayer or worship tradition. For this very reason attachment
to the person of Buddha was even more intense. He had no
rivals; he alone was the saviour-guide. During the early
centuries of Buddhism this profound attachment to Buddha
as a saviour-personality can be seen. It led immediately to
a type of devotion not far from worship. The people of India
at this time had no satisfactory devotional life. It is not
strange then that the stupas which enshrined the relics of
Buddha became centres of pilgrimage, that a devotional art
and literature appeared almost immediately.

The *Mahaparinirvana Sutra* mentions the worship ceremonies carried out at the time of Buddha's death. These
ceremonies were left to the lay people of Kushinagara. The
monks apparently took no part in them. Thus the devotional
development was from the beginning associated with the
laity. As more stupas were built, as the ceremonies were
enlarged, and as the devotional practises invaded the monasteries, the question arose as to the value of such religious,
or semireligious activities. This was discussed especially as
regards the devotional practise of gift-giving. One of the
propositions of the *Points of Controversy* states: "It should
not be said that anything given to the Buddha brings great
reward." The Theravada answered: "Was not the Exalted
One of all two-footed creatures the highest and best and
foremost and uttermost, supreme, unequalled, unrivalled,
peerless, incomparable, unique? How then could a gift to

him fail to bring great reward? Are there any equal to him in virtue, in will, in intellect?" (*Katha.* xvii, 10.)

The problem emerges in even greater detail in the *Questions of King Milinda.* Challenged as regards the titles of Buddha, Nagasena answers:

A king is one who is held worthy of homage by the multitudes who approach him, who come into his presence. And the Blessed One, O King, is held worthy of homage by multitudes of beings, whether gods or men, who approach him, who come into his presence. This too is the reason why the Tathagata is called a king. A king is one who, when pleased with a strenuous servant, gladdens his heart by bestowing upon him, at his own good pleasure, any costly gift the officer may choose. And the Blessed One, O King, when pleased with anyone who has been strenuous in word or deed or thought, gladdens his heart by bestowing upon him, as a selected gift, the supreme deliverance from all sorrow— far beyond all material gifts (*Mil.* 227).

This simple reasoning process to justify the intercommunion and exchange of gifts between Buddha and his followers expresses with great precision the change that was taking place in the Buddhist tradition. Release from sorrow is now seen as a gift from a person capable of bestowing such a sublime treasure. This is at an opposite extreme from the exhortation, "Work out your salvation with diligence."

Although the gift given does not benefit Buddha, it does benefit the giver of the gift. "If gods or men put up a building to contain the jewel treasure of the relics of a Tathagata who does not accept their gift, still by that homage paid to the attainment of the supreme good, under the form of the jewel treasure of his wisdom, they themselves attain to one or other of the three glorious states" (*Mil.* 96).

Once such a foundation for ceremonial and religious offerings had been established, a new period in Buddhist life was in process. This produced such elaborate festivals as those mentioned by the Buddhist pilgrims from China. Fa-

hsien mentions a prolonged period of Buddhist festival cele-
brated in the city of Khotan in the region of Chinese Turkes-
tan.

> The monks of the Gomati monastery, being Mahayana
> students, and held in greatest reverence by the king, took
> precedence of all the others in the procession. At a distance
> of over a mile from the city, they made a four-wheeled
> image car, more than thirty cubits high, which looked like a
> great hall of a monastery moving along. The seven precious
> substances were grandly displayed about it, with silken stream-
> ers and canopies hanging all around. The chief image stood
> in the middle of the car, with two Bodhisattvas in attendance
> on it, while degas were made to follow in waiting, all bril-
> liantly carved in gold and silver, and hanging in the air. When
> the car was a hundred paces from the gate, the king put off
> his crown of state, changed his dress for a fresh suit, and
> with bare feet, carrying in his hands flowers and incense,
> and with two rows of followers, went out at the gate to meet
> the image; and, with his face bowed to the ground, he did
> homage at its feet, and then scattered the flowers and burnt
> the incense. When the image was entering the gate, the queen
> and the brilliant ladies with her in the gallery above scat-
> tered far and wide all kinds of flowers, which floated about
> and fell promiscuously to the ground. In this way everything
> was done to promote the dignity of the occasion. The car-
> riages of the monasteries were all different, and each one
> had its own day for the procession. The ceremony began
> on the first day of the fourth month, and ended on the
> fourteenth, after which the king and queen returned to the
> palace (*Travels of Fa-hsien*, Ch. 3).

The burden of salvation was progressively shifted from
the initiative of man to the compassion of Buddha. The
work of man was no longer the intense moral effort of the
earlier period; it was rather a work of worship and devotional
practises. Many of these ceremonies were as elaborate as
that described above, but many, too, were reduced to the
simplest offerings and manifestations of reverence.

Even men and boys, who during the lesson or at play, as amusement, have drawn images upon the walls with the nail or with a piece of wood, have all reached enlightenment, they have become compassionate, and, by rousing many Bodhisattvas, have saved multitudes of creatures (*Lotus* ii, 86–87).

Those who offered flowers and perfumes to the relics of the Tathagatas, to stupas, a mound of earth, images of clay or drawn on a wall, who have caused musical instruments, drums, conch trumpets, and noisy great drums to be played, and raised the rattle of tymbals at such places in order to celebrate the highest enlightenment . . . they have all of them reached enlightenment (ii, 88–89).

Those who, when in the presence of a stupa, have offered their reverential salutation, be it in a complete form or by merely joining the hands; who, were it but for a single moment, bent their head or body; and who at stupas containing relics have one single time said: "Homage be to Buddha!" albeit they did it with distracted thoughts, all have attained superior enlightenment (ii, 94–95).

One of the highest forms of worship and devotion that developed at this time was the invocation of the sacred name of Buddha. This is particularly associated with Amitabha Buddha. The Mahayana scripture known as the *Land of Bliss Sutra* advocates this practise for the attainment of rebirth in Paradise. Amitabha preaches:

This prayer was mine formerly, so that beings having in any way whatever heard my name should for ever go to my country. And this my excellent prayer has been fulfilled, and beings having quickly come here from any worlds into my presence, never return from here, not even for one birth (*Sukhivativyuha* xxxi, 17).

See, O Ajita, what easy gains are gained by those beings who will hear the name of the Tathagata Amitabha, holy and fully enlightened. Nor will those beings be of little faith, who will obtain at least one joyful thought of that Tathagata and of this treatise of the Law. (*Sukhivativyuha*, xliii). . . . Every son or daughter of a family who shall hear the name of that repetition of the Law and retain in their memory the names of those blessed Buddhas, will be favoured by the Buddhas, and will never return again, being once in possession of the transcendent true knowledge. Therefore, O Sariputra, believe, accept, and do not doubt of me and those blessed Buddhas! (*Smaller Sukhivativyuha*, xvii.)

Not only does Buddha assume the burden of salvation and make this process as simple as possible for mankind, Buddha also wishes to drench the world and every living being in his mercy. As a great rain-cloud Buddha pours down a saving deluge upon all the earth:

It is, Kasyapa, as if a cloud rising above the horizon shrouds all space in darkness and covers the earth. That great rain-cloud, big with water, is wreathed with flashes of lightning and rouses with its thundering call all creatures. By warding off the sunbeams, it cools the region; and gradually lowering so as to come in reach of hands, it begins pouring down its water all around. And so, flashing on every side, it pours out an abundant mass of water equally, and refreshes this earth. And all herbs which have sprung up on the face of the earth, all grasses, shrubs, forest tree, other trees small and great; the various field fruits and whatever is green; all plants on hills, in caves and thickets. . . .

In the same way, Kasyapa, the Buddha comes into the world like a rain-cloud, and, once born, he, the world's Lord, speaks and shows the real course of life. The great Seer, honoured in the world, including the gods, speaks thus: I am the Tathagata, the highest of men, the Leader, I appear in this world like a cloud. I refresh all beings whose bodies are withered, who are clogged to the triple world. I bring to felicity those that are pining away with toils, give them pleasures and final rest. . . . I re-create the whole world like a cloud shedding its water without distinction; I have the same feelings for respectable people as for the low; for moral persons as for the immoral; for the depraved as for those who observe the rules of good conduct; for those who hold sectarian views and unsound tenets as for those whose views are sound and correct (*Lotus* v, 5–25).

This heavenly grace was the more needed since the Age of Corruption had begun. Only by heavenly merit could anyone be saved, merit evoked by the faith of the believer and rained down by the grace of the Buddha.

A very difficult work has been done by Sakyamuni, the sovereign of the Sakyas. Having obtained the transcendent true knowledge in this world Saha, he taught the Law which all the world is reluctant to accept, during this corruption of the present world-aeon, during this corruption of mankind, during this corruption of belief, during this corruption of life, during this corruption of passions (*Smaller Sukhivati-vyuha*, xviii).

This is one of the most important features of Mahayana Buddhism, the belief that the world was so changed that the type of salvation offered by the earlier Buddhism was no longer possible. The exhortation to strive earnestly was no longer effective. Salvation was no longer attainable by human effort. There were only faith and grace and heavenly providence. This must especially be kept in mind when reading the *Lotus Sutra*. The revelation of this Sutra supposedly took place at the time of Buddha's death, but it was not fully proclaimed until the period of wickedness had arrived. In answer to the address of the Lord during this last majestic discourse, the Bodhisattvas declared: "Be at ease, O Lord. After thy complete extinction, in the horrible last period of the world, we will proclaim this sublime Sutra (*Lotus*, xii, 2).

In greater detail the promise reveals:

Let the Lord be at ease in this respect; after the extinction of the Tathagata, we will expound this Sutra to all creatures, though we are aware, O Lord, that at that period there shall be malign beings, having few roots of goodness, conceited, fond of gain and honour, rooted in unholiness, difficult to tame, deprived of good will, and full of unwillingness. Nevertheless, O Lord, we will at that period read, keep, preach, write, honour, respect, venerate, worship this Sutra; with sacrifice of body and life, O Lord, we will divulge this Sutra. Let the Lord be at ease. . . . We will divulge this teaching of dharma after the complete extinction of the Lord, in the last days, the last period, though in other worlds. For in this Saha world, O Lord, creatures are conceited, possessed of few roots of goodness, always vicious in their thoughts, wicked, and naturally perverse (*Lotus* xii, Intro.).

Precisely at this time of corruption the higher way of perfection, the career of the Bodhisattva, and the higher goal, Buddhahood, are revealed. Also the highest wisdom is revealed, the wisdom that brings Buddhist thought to its meridian moment of grandeur.

CHAPTER XIV

HOMELESS WISDOM

Buddhism begins with dukkha (sorrow) and ends with prajna (wisdom). No abstract intellectual type of knowledge, this wisdom is a transforming enlightenment, an exalted, supreme, saving vision. It is much closer to religious experience than to any specific form of knowledge according to our usual categories.

The higher wisdom of Mahayana Buddhism is an overwhelming subject, vast in its scope, sublime in its basic insight. The literature on this subject, in its quality, volume and influence can be considered the most significant body of spiritual and intellectual literature ever produced in the Far-Asian world. It is spread over four major languages—Sanskrit, Tibetan, Chinese and Japanese—and several less important languages of central Asia.

The wisdom aspect of Mahayana Buddhism is more significant than the devotional aspect. A supreme liberating vision is the end and purpose of devotional Buddhism. Final bliss itself is considered an intellectual awakening from illusion to reality. Even in the *Land of Bliss Sutra* we read of those born in Paradise that their final attainment is "transcendental wisdom." "They discard the eye of flesh, and assume the heavenly eye. Having approached the eye of wisdom, having reached the eye of the dharma, producing the eye of Buddha, showing it, illumining and fully exhibiting it, they attain perfect wisdom" (*Sukhivativyuha Sutra* xxxi, 38).

So important is wisdom in the Mahayana tradition that

all major Mahayana scriptures may be considered wisdom scriptures. All are concerned with prajna and the methods of its attainment. Even the *Lotus Sutra* holds forth enlightenment as the very essence of Buddhahood. There Buddha himself announces that he preaches only the Buddha vehicle that "leads to omniscience" (ii, 36). The Bodhisattvas all exclaim: "May we also become such incomparable Buddhas in the world, who by mysterious speech announce supreme Buddha-enlightenment" (iii, 37). The parable of the Burning House has for its purpose the bringing of mankind to supreme enlightenment. The father of the children says: "Truly, I am the father of these beings; I must save them from this mass of evil, and bestow on them the immense, inconceivable bliss of Buddha-knowledge, wherewith they shall sport, play and divert themselves, wherein they shall find their rest" (*Lotus* iii, 38).

But while all Mahayana scriptures may be considered to have wisdom as their central theme, there are a group of almost forty Sutras that bear the specific name of Wisdom Books. These works, which present the higher wisdom of Mahayana Buddhism, were composed apparently between 100 B.C. and A.D. 100. Afterwards, from A.D. 200 to A.D. 700 the great creative masters of Mahayana developed this wisdom tradition in a massive *Shastra* literature. This Wisdom Literature was then completed by commentators who wrote from about A.D. 400 until around A.D. 1200 in India, China, Tibet, and Japan. Since that time there has been a continuing tradition of Mahayana scholarship in Tibet and also to some extent in China and Japan.

Of the Wisdom Literature properly so called, the *Prajnaparamita Sutras,* the central work is the *Wisdom Sutra in 8,000 Verses.* This was enlarged in various proportions until it attained in one version some 100,000 verses. Then the whole mass of the material was reduced to some score of pages in the *Diamond Sutra,* to a few paragraphs in the *Heart Sutra.* For its concentrated expression of a vast and complex intellectual and spiritual experience, the *Heart Sutra* belongs among the most impressive works produced by man. This brief expression of the higher Buddhist wisdom is centred on an intense effort to get beyond the world of names and forms.

The sublime Lord, Avalokita, the Bodhisattva, moving in the profound ways of Perfect Wisdom, looked down from above, saw the five manifestations of reality, and perceived that they were empty in their very being.

O! Shariputra, here form is emptiness, emptiness is form. Form differs not from emptiness. Emptiness differs not from form. That which is emptiness, that is form. That which is form that is emptiness. The same is to be said of feelings, perceptions, mental-formations, and consciousness.

Here, Shariputra, all things are characterized by emptiness. They do not come into being or cease to be. They are neither impure nor pure, neither imperfect nor perfect. Therefore, Shariputra, there are in emptiness no forms, no feelings, no perceptions, no mental-formation, no consciousness.

There is no eye, ear, nose, tongue, body, mind. No form, sound, smell, taste, touch, or objects. There is no organ of sight and so forth until we come to: There is no knowledge, no ignorance, and no destruction of ignorance, and so forth, until we come to: no decay and death, no destruction of decay and death.

There is no sorrow, no origination of sorrow, no cessation of sorrow, no path to cessation of sorrow. There is no knowledge; there is neither attainment, nor nonattainment.

Thus, Shariputra, because of his nonattainment the Bodhisattva, relying on Perfect Wisdom, dwells without thought-obstruction. Because of this freedom from thought-obstruction he is free from all fear, he is beyond change, he reaches final Nirvana.

All the Buddhas of the past, present and future, after attaining this supreme wisdom, are fully awakened in the final, complete and Perfect Wisdom.

Therefore one should know the great magic verse of Perfect Wisdom, the supreme verse, the unsurpassed verse, the sublime verse which soothes all sorrow—for it is truth, not illusion, the verse proclaimed by Perfect Wisdom: Gone, gone, gone beyond, gone entirely beyond. Such an awakening! Svaha!

The most significant word in this short treatise on wisdom is the word *svabhavasunya*, which means "empty in its own being." This applies first to form, then to all the other four manifestations of physical and psychical phenomena as they appear to us. This word *sunya*, which means "empty," also appears in the abstract noun form as *sunyata* or "emptiness." This supreme word in the higher wisdom of Buddhism is the final designation of phenomenal reality. When we truly understand reality, when we see into its depths, we find *sunyata*.

When Western thinkers look at the phenomenal world they see what is there. When Buddhist thinkers look at the phenomenal world they see what is not there. The spirituality needed to deal with this situation has for its purpose the liberation of mankind from entanglement in this world that appears real but which in reality is only emptiness. The *Diamond Sutra* ends with the verse:

> As stars, darkness, a lamp,
> A phantom, dew, a bubble,
> A dream, a flash of lightning, a cloud,
> Thus should we look upon the world.

This vision, that things are insubstantial, that they are empty in their very being, is a vision attained only from above, from the heights of a wisdom higher than that ordinarily attained by man. In the first verse of the *Heart Sutra* there is mention that Avalokita, the Bodhisattva, looked down from above. From this lofty view of Perfect Wisdom he saw that all things were empty in their own being. The remainder of the Sutra is the detailed application of this designation to all the Buddhist categories of psychic and physical phenomena. Supreme enlightenment consists in getting beyond all of these things to the enlightenment that is "without thought-covering." Our sensual, intellectual, and emotional processes impede rather than aid our final full awakening. Emergence into a higher experience inevitably brings about submergence of a lower experience.

The final expression of the *Heart Sutra* is the exclamation: "Gone, gone, gone beyond, gone completely beyond. Such an wakening! Svaha!" This awakening must be understood as a transition from illusion to reality. It is not a vision of something. It is a final release from all that keeps man from the going-over. This Sutra has no satisfactory word for what is attained beyond by this passage. With a certain deliberate care it limits itself to a description of the receding shore of this world which now is seen as *sunyata,* emptiness.

From the very beginning Buddhism was striving for this moment, the meridian moment of Buddhist intellectual and spiritual development, the moment when it could utter the word *sunyata* with such depth of meaning. Yet awareness that all things are empty is everywhere present in the earlier Buddhism. It was present when all things of the phenomenal world were seen as transient, sorrowful, insubstantial.

Anicca, which designates the transient nature of things, is the first Buddhist insight into *sunyata.* Perception of change led Western thought to consideration of the unmoved mover of things in the cosmological process. Eventually this process of reasoning was taken up and made a principle for identification of an eternal self-existent being, the unmoved being upon whom all motion depends, the point whence all motion has its origin and end. Motion or change was the manifestation of reality emerging from a primordial source of being.

But the perception of transient reality in the Buddhist world led to a vision of the nothingness of all things that come into existence and pass out of existence. The impermanence of things is seen as emptiness.

The second quality of things, *dukkha,* the painful aspect of things, led to the concept of *sunyata* in a somewhat different way. When man grasped transient things to satisfy desire, he found that things dissolved in his grasp and completely failed to bestow what was desired. This sorrow only increased with further efforts towards satisfaction in the empty things of the surrounding world. Thus man not only became aware that things were empty; he was thrown into emotional and mental agony by the experience of this nothingness.

It was only under the pressure of such agony that any true depth of Buddhist insight became possible. This unrelieved tension drove man not only into the awareness that all things were empty in their very being but to a doctrine giving expression to this emptiness. If in Buddhist India there had been no such extraordinary sensitivity to sorrow, the disciples of Buddha might never have emerged from the limited insights of the Hinayana schools of Buddhism. The experience of sorrow must be recognized as the foundation of the intellectual processes of Buddhism. These pressures created spiritual tensions that sought release in total liberation. When the experience of *sunyata* was attained, then all tensions were dissolved, desire disappeared, peace was gained. An ultimate wisdom had liberated man from the primeval sorrow of life.

This final wisdom might be considered the going forth of the mind into the homeless state. The experience of *sunyata* is the final culmination, the fulfilment of the age-old quest of India that from the earliest times led men forth from home into the homeless state.

This going forth from the status of householder to become a wandering recluse is found nowhere else in the higher civilizations of the Eurasian world. Yet in India it has always been a normal, an accepted thing. If the spiritual personality of India is emotionally not fully at rest in the ordinary life

of home and family, so also spiritually the mind of India is
not entirely at home in its own thoughts. There is a longing
in both instances for some more satisfying experience that is
obstructed by living in the ordinary ways of mankind. The
intellectual culture of India no less than the religious culture
of India is best expressed by this going forth from home.

This going forth into the homeless state involved a renunciation much more absolute than is generally realized.
In Hindu tradition, not only are material possessions renounced along with a permanent abode, not only does a person separate himself from his family, relatives, and friends;
a person also separates himself from religious rituals, sacred
texts, and holy symbols. Sacraments and sacramentals, sacred texts and ceremonies, are considered to be a final en-
cumbrance that hinders man in his quest for the reality of
what is signified by these sacred signs and ceremonies. A
person must, in the last stages of perfection, pass from symbol to reality. This transition is itself symbolized in ceremonial form. Thus we have a ritual renunciation of ritual, as
in the beginning there was a ritual entry into a ritual pattern
of life. In the Hindu ritual for the going forth, a person
symbolically takes up the sacred fire into himself by bending
over the fire for the last time, breathing the fire into his
own being. Then he consumes a handful of ashes from the
embers. Most significant of all he takes off the sacred cord,
the symbol of his second birth, his spiritual birth into Hinduism. This and a lock of his hair are buried in the earth or
sunk into water. Removal of the sacred cord indicates the
abandonment of Hinduism itself. The giving up of the lock
of hair indicates the renunciation of all earthly and family
relations. The last thing renounced is the son who accom-
panies the newly dedicated Sannyasin for a short distance
where they turn around and separate from each other without looking back. Thus Hinduism goes forth out of itself.

All of these things that take place in the going forth of
the Sannyasin, this going forth into the homeless life, take

place intellectually in the Buddhist traditions of India. The Buddhist, however, is less interested in the giving up of religious ceremonies. He gave these up when he first became a Buddhist. He is much more interested in abandonment of the mental and emotional bonds with the transient, sorrowful, insubstantial world. This clings in the mind even when it is abandoned externally. The difficulty of attaining the final disengagement, that is what is dealt with in the wisdom literature of Mahayana Buddhism. This is the meaning of the *Heart Sutra.* It describes the going forth of the mind into the world of complete emptiness, a world without thought-covering or thought-obstacle, because thought itself has been abandoned.

It is not surprising that this mental going forth was at first attained only by those who had physically and emotionally gone forth from home and family. For the mind to live without its possessions of ideas and thoughts, without the support and nourishment proper to it, this is an achievement of some stature. It required a training that reached deep into the physical, emotional, and psychic life as well as into the intellectual and spiritual life.

It is particularly significant that the *Heart Sutra,* the most concise expression of the doctrine of sunyata, is also the Sutra in which Buddhism negates itself and the Buddhist mind goes forth from itself into total homelessness. Thus the Four Noble Truths of Buddhism and the Eightfold Path are denied. "There is no sorrow, no origination of sorrow, no cessation of sorrow, no Eightfold Path to the cessation of sorrow." Prior to his negation of the Four Noble Truths and the Eightfold Path there had been a negation of the original intuition of Buddha expressed in the doctrine of Dependent Origination: "There is no knowledge, no ignorance, and no destruction of ignorance, and so forth, until we come to: no decay and death, no destruction of decay and death." In the original teaching of Buddha the clinging to the world was associated with ignorance which brought into existence all attachments and resulted in the entire life process ending in decay and death. This in turn produced a new birth. The unending cycle continued until the final renunciation which enabled a person to escape from this terrifying cycle of existence. Now in the new Buddhism all this is denied as itself illusion. Ignorance itself is denied. In this denial there is a Buddhist going forth from Buddhism.

The result is attainment of a state wherein the mind is freed from obstacles that come from within the doctrine, as well as from obstacles that come from without. The mind escapes from the limitations constituted by the very doctrine of Buddhism. Adherence to Buddhist doctrine is itself a hindrance. These doctrines were valid only while the mind dwelt in the world of names and forms. After the transition was made into the world of sunyata, then Buddhist doctrine itself ceases to be of value. It also is emptiness. It also is a hindrance.

At an earlier moment in Buddhism this rejection of the Buddhist dharma by Buddhism had been described under the form of the raft. A man is described as having come to a stream of turbulent waters where there was no boat for crossing over. Considering the situation he says:

Suppose that I, having collected grass, sticks, branches and foliage, having tied a raft, depending on that raft, and striving with hands and feet, should cross over safely to the beyond? Then, monks, that man, having collected grass, sticks, branches and foliage, having tied a raft, depending on that raft and striving with his hands and feet, might cross over safely to the beyond. To him, crossed over, gone beyond, this might occur: "Now, this raft has been very useful to me. I, depending on this raft, and striving so with my hands and feet, crossed over safely to the beyond. Suppose now that I, having put this raft on my head, or having lifted it on to my shoulder, should proceed as I desire?" What do you think about this, monks? If that man does this, is he doing what should be done with that raft? "No, Lord."

What should that man do, monks, in order to do what should be done with that raft? In this case, monks, it might occur to that man who has crossed over, gone beyond: "Now, this raft has been very useful to me. Depending on this raft and striving with my hands and feet, I have crossed over safely to the beyond. Suppose now that I, having beached this raft on dry ground or having submerged it under the water, should proceed as I desire?" In doing this, monks, that man would be doing what should be done with that raft. Even so, monks, is the parable of the Raft Dharma taught by me for crossing over, not for retaining. You, monks, by understanding the parable of the raft, should leave the right way behind, even more the wrong way (*Maj.* i, 135).

But while there is such total abandonment of this world of name and form, there is, surprisingly enough, a final recovery of the world transformed in this higher wisdom of Buddhism. The world is recovered not in its original status but in a new modality. For if all things are sunya in their very being, then in possessing this intuition of sunyata a person attains the world of Samsara as well as the world of Nirvana. This is the most subtle, most difficult moment in the entire development of Buddhist thought. Comprehension of this moment challenges the deepest resources of the human mind. Yet without this comprehension, the last full expansion of Buddhist thought is lost to view.

The *Lotus Sutra* had proclaimed: "The Tathagata sees the triple world as it really it: it is not born, it dies not; it is not conceived, it springs not into existence; it moves not in a whirl, it becomes not extinct; it is not real, nor unreal; it is not existing, nor nonexisting; it is not such, nor otherwise, nor false" (*Lotus* xv, Introd.). Nagarjuna, in his famous *Karikas,* takes up this theme and writes:

> If Nirvana is neither being nor nonbeing
> No one can really understand

The teaching that proclaims at once
The negation of both.

After attaining Nirvana, what is Buddha?
Does he exist, does he not exist,
Is it both, or neither?
We will never understand it.

What, then, is Buddha even during his lifetime?
Does he exist, does he not exist,
Is it both, or neither?
We will never understand it.

This has taken the problem a step further by pointing out the mystery of earthly existence. This is as mysterious as, or even more mysterious than, transearthly existence. In this mystery, then, we have a type of unity that binds the two worlds together. It is this mystery that is indicated by the word *sunyata*. This leads, then, to a further step towards final unity of all things. This unity is stated with shocking abruptness by Nagarjuna. In these verses of his, *Samsara* designates the phenomenal or the conditioned world; *Nirvana* designates the transcendent, the unconditioned world.

There is really no difference
Between Nirvana and Samsara.
There is really no difference
Between Samsara and Nirvana.

That which defines Nirvana
Also defines Samsara.
Between these two we cannot find
Even a slight difference.

The two shores are no longer two shores, there is no longer the turbulent stream of time distinct from the distant shore. There is only the blissful mystery empty of all that men can really explain.

Within this mystery the world is lifted up towards the

transearthly, while this in turn descends to become as ordinary as daily life, as common as "carrying water and chopping wood." Indeed the difference between chopping wood and quiet meditation ceases to exist. Both become spiritual disciplines, ways of perfection, even the very same way of perfection. The sublime and the lowly meet in the one reality of simple human living. Thus the verse attributed to the Zen master, P'ang.

> How wondrously supernatural!
> How marvellous this!
> I draw water, I carry wood!
> (Suzuki, *Essays in Zen Buddhism*, iii, 87)

Vimalikirti marks one of the stages in advance to this position. His work, or the work known under this title, the *Teachings of Vimalikirti,* is one of the most crucial of all Mahayana scriptures for comprehending this phase of Buddhist thought. This work was never fully appreciated in India. It took the Chinese insight fully to appreciate the teachings of this work. It was the genius of Vimalikirti to establish the going forth into the homeless life without leaving home. This particularly fascinated the Chinese. Favourite themes in their paintings and stone engravings were the scenes of Vimalikirti preaching and carrying on discussion with the Bodhisattva, Manjusri.

Vimalikirti had an extraordinary capacity to live within rowful, but he voluntarily assumes existences in the conditioned and the unconditioned. Thus he says of the Bodhisattva: "He considers that all conditioned beings are sorrowful, but he voluntarily assumes existences in the conditioned world of Samsara" (*Vim.* x, 18). He saw that only those who have never left home have really left home. Those who have truly left home spiritually have nothing to gain by leaving home. They can safely and profitably remain at home. The classical description of Vimalikirti tells us:

He wears the white robe of the layman, but he conducts himself as a religious.

He dwells at home, yet he keeps himself free of sensuous desire.

Surrounded by servants, he constantly seeks after solitude.

Although adorned with ornaments, he is distinguished by spiritual simplicity.

While partaking of food and drink, he is nourished always with the savour of ecstatic insight.

He appears frequently in gambling houses but always to protect those attached to such amusements (*Vim.* ii, 3).

In his own description of the Bodhisattva, Vimalikirti tells us:

He associates constantly with the weak, the suffering, the miserable; yet he is handsome to look at and possesses a bodily splendour equal to that of Narayana.

He is found in the midst of wealth, yet he is without cupidity and he often meditates on the notion of impermanence.

He is associated with the destinies of the entire world, but he escapes the destinies of all.

He follows the way of Nirvana, but he does not abandon the way of Samsara" (*Vim.* vii, i).

CHAPTER XV

THE NEW SCRIPTURES

The new Buddhism produced a new literature. This literature can be divided into three major divisions: The scriptures proper, the early expositions of the scriptures by the great Mahayana masters, the later scholastic studies and commentaries. These latter studies were associated with the different schools of thought that emerged from within the Mahayana tradition.

There has never been any clearly established or separate canon of Mahayana scriptures. The Mahayana writings were never fixed in the definitive manner of the Hinayana scriptures that are preserved for us in the Pali language. Works were being added throughout the first four centuries of the Christian period. Some acquired greater authority within certain schools of Mahayana thought. Others were favoured in other schools. No one was concerned with establishing a definitive collection that would be accepted by all followers of the Mahayana. The tradition itself contained a number of disparate elements that developed from different sources independent of each other. These elements gradually attained integration in various schools of thought, principally through the Madhyamika school founded by Nagarjuna and the Yogacara School founded by Asanga and Vasubandhu. Asanga was particularly concerned with the orderly exposition of the Mahayana doctrines, but even he made no effort to identify any set group of works as the Mahayana canon.

The language of the Mahayana scriptures was Sanskrit, the learned language of India during this period. Buddhist writings in Sanskrit ranged from excellent literary Sanskrit, such as is found in Ashvaghosa, to a type of mixed Sanskrit and Prakrit which has recently been called Buddhist Hybrid Sanskrit. The classical Sanskrit language was just attaining its definitive form during the early Christian period.

Although an extensive volume of Buddhist literature was written in Sanskrit during these centuries, only a small proportion of this literature has been handed down to us in the Sanskrit language. Thankfully some of the most important of the Mahayana Sutras are among those that have survived. The Sanskrit documents that we now possess were discovered outside India. Most of these were found in Nepal, the place of refuge for Buddhist monks, their doctrines, and their writings during the period when Buddhism was being eliminated from India around the year A.D. 1000 and the centuries immediately after this date. But while a limited number of the Mahayana scriptures have survived in Sanskrit, a great number of works have survived in translation, mainly in Chinese and Tibetan. The Tibetan translations are especially important, since the Tibetans were more consistent in translating Sanskrit Buddhist terms than were the Chinese. In China there was never any fixed way of translating the technical terms of the Sanskrit. Thus in restoring the original text for the purpose of a more precise understanding of Buddhist works, the Tibetan is frequently of greater help than the Chinese.

Yet many of the Chinese translations were done with a genius of the first order. All types of Buddhist literature were translated, everything from basic scriptures to later studies and commentaries—anything expounding the doctrine, anything an aid to enlightenment. Altogether some 173 translators from Sanskrit into Chinese are known to us. Out of 3,283 Buddhist works in the Taisho edition of the Chinese Buddhist canon, some 1,691 works were translations. This constitutes a volume of translation unequalled in the history of cultural diffusion until modern times.

A large number of Mahayana works have appeared in Tibetan. These translations into Tibetan took place from the eighth century onwards. Of the fundamental scriptures of Buddhism that were translated into Tibetan, some two-thirds is Mahayana in content. There we find such works as the *Lalitavistara, Sukhivativyuha, Saddharmapundarika, Samdhinirmocana, Lankavatara, Mahaparinirvana, Karunapundarika,* and the *Samadhiraja Sutras.*

The authors of the Mahayana scriptures are unknown to us. We are not even certain when these scriptures were composed. The evidence is that they were for the most part composed in the period that begins with the first century B.C. and ends with the fourth century A.D. The *Wisdom Sutras* seem to have their earliest beginnings in the last part of the pre-Christian period. The *Lotus Sutra,* one of the most fundamental and one that gives evidence of early composition, was certainly completed by the year 200, although it is difficult to fix the precise time of its composition. Our best evidence for the time of composition of Mahayana Sutras comes from our knowledge of the time when these writings were first translated into Chinese. In most instances we have clear evidence of the time of translation of the Chinese texts.

The Mahayana scriptures claim to be the very words of Buddha himself or the doctrine of Buddha as spoken by one of the Bodhisattvas. The time and place are given to identify the occasion, supposedly during the lifetime of Buddha, on which the scripture was communicated. As with the Hinayana scriptures, so with the Mahayana, they begin with the same introductory phrase, "Thus have I heard." Since the Buddha of the Mahayanists is less historical than the Buddha of the Hinayana, the scriptural setting is sometimes more celestial than earthly. The Buddha in his Celestial or Sambhoga Body is presented as surrounded by the company of heavenly

Bodhisattvas as well as by a vast assembly on earth. The revelation given in this setting is considered of greater significance than the revelation given while Buddha appeared merely in his Transformation Body.

While there is no satisfactory or complete listing of the Mahayana scriptures, we give here some that are of special importance. These might well claim the attention of anyone who wishes to know something of Mahayana Buddhism from its basic texts. These have been chosen for their intrinsic importance, for the influence they have had on the course of Mahayana development, and for their availability in Western languages.

1. There is first the *Lotus Sutra,* known as the *Saddharmapundarika Sutra,* that is, *The Lotus of the True Law Sutra.* This Sutra, written prior to A.D. 200, is the most renowned of the Mahayana Sutras, especially in the East Asian world of China, Korea, and Japan. It is a book so sacred that it is itself given a veneration that amounts to worship. Salvation is promised to all those who honour the Sutra, to all who cause it to be known and honoured by others. The Buddha presence is felt in this work more than in any other single work of the Mahayana. The revelation is supposedly given on a mountain near Rajagriha where Buddha has gone just before his final passing from the phenomenal world into Nirvana. Pictured with apocalyptic grandeur at this moment, he is surrounded by infinite numbers of monks and the faithful, and by the glorious Bodhisattvas. His own body is so resplendent that it illumines the entire cosmos. There he reveals the most significant communication ever made to mankind, the glory of the Buddhas of all past ages and the glory of Buddhahood that awaits all mankind in the future.

There is only this one way of salvation from the destructive elements of life, the way of Buddhahood, not the way of Nirvana. All past revelations concerning the Arhat ideal of perfection were only temporary expedients given to a mankind that was as yet not prepared for the sublime vocation of Buddhahood. That this involves a decisive break with the Hinayana tradition is insisted on throughout the *Lotus Sutra*. The Arhat ideal, the Nirvana goal, the nature of reality, all of these fundamental elements in the Hinayana are now seen in a new light and come under a new critique.

To explain this new ideal a number of parables are told, parables that are among the greatest and best known in Buddhist tradition, the parables of the Burning House, the Lost Son, and the Good Physician. To understand these parables is to have an excellent beginning towards understanding Mahayana Buddhism. In each of these instances something is offered mankind that is too sublime for understanding. To the children in the burning house toys are offered if they will come outside and escape from the fire that is destroying the dwelling. But the gifts given when they emerge are not toys, they are real treasures. So with the other parables. The higher destiny of man is too sublime for understanding. Man must be seduced to a better life by the attraction of what he can already understand and desire. This is not really deception. It is the communication of truth according to the capacity of the one receiving it.

Behind this entire process is the sublime compassion of the Buddha. The grandeur, the tenderness of his concern for the welfare of mankind, is beyond comprehension. This is the secret of the vast influence that the *Lotus Sutra* has had on the Asian world. It provided mankind with the highest goal reached by the simplest means. It also gave to man the spiritual assurance of emerging out of the sorrows of time into the bliss of Buddhahood. Invocation of the name of Buddha, honouring the *Lotus Sutra,* drawing an image of the Buddha in the sand, any single deed of man done with devotion for Buddha sufficed for salvation. Even in this life such people would share in the protection of the Bodhisattva Avalokitesvara. A single cry directed to him when in the midst of danger or suffering would bring immediate release:

Those who shall keep the name of this Bodhisattva Mahasattva Avalokitesvara, young man of good family, will, if they fall into a great mass of fire, be delivered therefrom by virtue of the lustre of the Bodhisattva Mahasattva. In case, young man of good family, creatures, carried off by the current of rivers, should implore the Bodhisattva Mahasattva Avalokitesvara, all rivers will provide them a ford. . . . If a man given up to capital punishment implores Avalokitesvara, the swords of the executioners shall snap asunder. . . . If some creatures shall be bound in wooden or iron manacles, chains or fetters, be he guilty or innocent, then those manacles, chains or fetters shall give way as soon as the name of the Bodhisattva Mahasattva Avalokitesvara is pronounced. Such, young man of good family, is the power of the Bodhisattva Mahasattva Avalokitesvara. . . . Think, O think, with tranquil mood of Avalokitesvara, that pure being; he is a protector, a refuge, a recourse in death, disaster, and calamity (*Lotus Sutra* xxiv).

2. The *Wisdom Sutras,* the *Prajnaparamita Sutra.* This title includes an entire class of writings concerned with the ultimate nature of reality and the manner in which this can be thought and expressed by the human mind. As with most mystical traditions, the wisdom tradition of Mahayana Buddhism tends strongly towards negative modalities of expression. The central word of the *Wisdom Sutras* is *sunyata,* "emptiness." All things are void of reality; all things, all thoughts, all expressions. The great dilemmas involved in dealing with the phenomenal world are brought out in this process of inquiry, which is the most fundamental inquiry ever made by Buddhism into both the objective and subjective worlds. As Hinduism came to the conception of Brahman by its observation of the world without and to the conception of Atman by awareness of the world within the mind, Buddhism came in both instances to a profound experience of *sunyata,* emptiness.

The expression of this new intellectual experience is contained in some forty *Wisdom Sutras* written over a period of a thousand years, from the first century B.C. to the tenth century A.D. There was first a period when the fundamental text was established around the beginning of the Christian period. This was the *Wisdom Sutra in 8,000 Lines*. Then for several centuries there were a number of expanded versions of this original work, in 25,000, 80,000 and 100,000 lines. Then came a number of smaller versions that reduced the text to 700 lines, to a few chapters, and finally to a few paragraphs. Later, beginning with the seventh century, a number of Tantric versions were produced that turned these Sutras into magical formulas. According to the most eminent English scholar of the Wisdom Literature, Edward Conze, sixteen texts belong to the non-Tantric schools; twenty-four texts belong to the Tantric school. Most of these latter are rather brief. Although some of the Tantras are of great importance in the study of the spiritual and intellectual history of mankind, they have as yet been little studied in the Western world.

These *Wisdom Sutras* provided the impetus for a vast intellectual expansion within the Buddhist tradition. All later development of thought within the Mahayana depends on these works for their basic foundations. Both the principal schools of Mahayana, the Madhyamika and the Yogacara, depend upon the *Wisdom Sutras* for their original vision, even though these two schools developed this original tradition in different directions, one through the use of logical processes, the other through a psychological analysis made by the intellect of its own functioning.

The essential teaching of the *Wisdom Sutras* can be found in the 8,000-line Sutra and in the two shorter works, the *Diamond Sutra* and the *Heart Sutra*. This last work is of special importance, for it has condensed a vast amount of thought and meditation on the deepest mysteries of reality into a few short paragraphs. To understand this Sutra, however, requires a basic acquaintance with the entire Buddhist tradition, especially with the Abhidharma tradition of Hinayana Buddhism. The other relatively short work, the *Diamond Sutra,* attracted most attention from Buddhist thinkers of the East Asian world. Both the *Heart Sutra* and the *Diamond Sutra* expound the same basic ideas, that the world of reality about us is only a world of appearance, a magical illusion, a dream, an insubstantial cloud, a bubble that bursts and disappears in an instant, a drop of dew that dissolves in the sunlight. The *Diamond Sutra* gives forceful expression to the inadequacies and contradictions involved in any intellectual position. All this is presented, however, rather as a device for forcing the mind to a higher nonconceptual experience than to demonstrate a nihilistic attitude towards the world.

Until the recent work of Edward Conze appeared, very little of this Wisdom Literature was available to the Western world. The *Diamond* and the *Heart Sutras* had been translated by Max Müller and published in the Sacred Books of the East Series, but there was little real understanding even of these works. It has required the intellectual experience that the West has gone through in the mid-twentieth century to prepare the way for understanding the type of intellectual experience presented in these works. Now a sizable body of texts and studies is available. These are especially important for understanding the background of Zen Buddhism.

3. The *Avatamsaka Sutra.* Here again we have a group of Sutras rather than a single work organized in systematic fashion. A number of different works were incorporated into this one Sutra. Some of these, especially the *Gandavyuha* and the *Dasabhumika,* still exist as independent works. Yet all of these should be considered together, for they have the same essential message, that of the final cosmic identity. This is the doctrine that all reality is contained in each of its parts, even the smallest. This work has a special feeling for the doctrine that transcendence and immanence are one and the same thing. They must not be thought of apart from each other.

The whole of this Sutra is found in three different versions of varying length in Chinese translation; in eighty, sixty, and forty fascicles. One of these, the one in forty fascicles, is known as the *Gandavyuha Sutra*. Another that belongs to this collection is the *Dasabhumika*. The *Avatamsaka* collection contains some of the most significant of all Buddhist teachings. It is also one of the most difficult to deal with because of the general elevation of its thought. It has been considered by some scholars of China and Japan as the greatest of all the Mahayana Sutras in the sublimity of its teaching, both because of its treatment of cosmic identity and because of the emotional and affective qualities that it combines with this high intellectualism. It brings heaven to earth in a manner seldom realized in the religious literature of the world. This is the moment when Buddhism seemed to have the vision described by Dante when he wrote in the *Divine Comedy* after his vision of Divine Reality that he had seen therein "All the scattered leaves of the universe bound by love in one volume" (Par. xxxiii, p. 85). The *Avatamsaka* combines the compassion of the *Lotus Sutra* with the intellectualism of the *Wisdom Sutras*. Its spiritual depth of feeling makes it a religious classic. Its intellectual insight makes it a work of great philosophical significance.

Because this Sutra has been studied very little in the West, its true understanding must await the work of scholars who will give to it the attention that other scholars such as Sylvain Lévi, Louis De La Vallée-Poussin, Étienne Lamotte, Edward Conze and Guiseppi Tucci have given to other Sutras and Shastras of Mahayana traditions. The *Gandavyuha* section of this Sutra will provide an exceptional experience for the West when it is made available. This is the story of the highest of man's spiritual efforts ever made in the Mahayana tradition. It leads to the awareness that the transcendent world of Nirvana is not different from the immanent world of Samsara. Here we have the ending of the quest of Buddhism which was originally evoked by the experience of dukkha, of sorrow, in the world of change and the rejection of this world as transient, painful, and insubstantial. Now Buddhism comes to the end of its quest in the *Gandavyuha Sutra*. A complete transformation of reality has taken place. An entirely different world has emerged, a kind of resurrected world, a world not despised and rejected but elevated and glorified into a condition of bliss. Both wisdom and love, *prajna* and *karuna,* have attained their completion.

The other section of the *Avatamsaka* that has had such great influence in western Asia is the *Dasabhumika,* the Sutra of the Ten Stages of development in the career of a Bodhisattva. These stages, which later became an integral part of the Mahayana Buddhism, are stages of spiritual perfection which end in supreme bliss.

4. The *Vimalikirti Sutra, Vimalikirtinirdesa.* While the *Avatamsaka Sutra* has a cosmic quality that is unique among the Mahayana Sutras, the *Vimalikirti Sutra* has a domestic aspect that provides its distinctive quality. Not that this Sutra is less sublime in its thought. It is indeed one of the most exalted of all the Sutras. It combines a lofty spiritual insight with the life of an ordinary householder in the midst of worldly affairs. A superb humanism marks this work. Vimalikirti not only lives in the midst of the world, he enjoys life. He even has delight and a certain amount of fun in seeing the world from his highly spiritual point of view. The spiritual personality belongs in the world of man if he is going to communicate salvation to man. Thus we have again the union of high intellectual vision with a depth of emotional feeling.

Because of the identity with the world that marks this Sutra, it is one of the finest of the Mahayana Sutras in its literary style. There is, here, none of the strain of exaggeration found in those Sutras where the author himself seems to be still on the quest for wisdom. The *Vimalikirti Sutra* is written by someone who has already acquired the perfection of vision and is no longer striving. Thus he can write with assurance, ease, simplicity, and a certain playfulness. He understands great paradoxes of reality and responds to them with delight. He lives in the world of the transcendent and yet in the world of change, in the world of nonduality and yet in the world of duality. This incongruity provides wonderful material for quiet amusement. If Vimalikirti is presented as one ill, speaking from a sick bed, he is indeed the only one truly well. Yet he must appear ill to achieve identity with those still struggling towards a life of virtue.

Doctrinally this Sutra is dominated by the concepts of emptiness and nonduality.

> Matter is empty; it is not by the destruction of matter that it is empty; the very nature of matter is emptiness. Likewise to speak of sensation, idea, volition, and knowledge, on the one hand, and of emptiness, on the other, that makes a duality. But knowledge is empty; it is not by the destruction of knowledge that it is empty; the very nature of knowledge is its emptiness. Whoever sees the five clusters which evoke attachment and so understands them by knowledge, enters into nonduality (*Vim.* viii, 17).

This principle is applied to all the apparent realities of both the objective and subjective works. Final release from the restrictions and sorrows of the perishable world is attained only by the vision that passes beyond all multiplicity and all division.

This Sutra, among the most ancient of the Mahayana Sutras, comes down to us from the period just after the composition of the *Wisdom Sutras*. It is certainly prior to the third century. The Sanskrit texts have all disappeared, but the work is preserved in Chinese and Tibetan translations. It was translated into Chinese by Kumarajiva in the fifth century A.D. and by Hsüan-tsang in the seventh century. The translation of Kumarajiva has a literary quality that makes it more readable than the translation of Hsüan-tsang, although the latter is the one most faithful to the original and provides our best text for translation into Western languages.

This work has always been a favourite text in China and Japan. In China it provided an ideal of perfection that suited the humanist type of scholar who carried on the intellectual and spiritual traditions of that country. Through their own Taoist traditions the Chinese had already undergone extensive preparation for understanding and enjoying the paradoxes of Vimalikirti.

5. The *Explanation of Mysteries Sutra,* the *Samhinirmocana Sutra.* If some of the earlier *Wisdom Sutras* give a certain obscurity to the Mahayana teaching by constantly stating the doctrine in enigmatic terms, this Sutra produces a clear and precise understanding of the doctrine with little obscurity. It was composed very early in the Mahayana period, just after the *Wisdom Sutras,* approximately at the time when the *Vimalikirti* and *Lankavatara Sutras* were being written. It is an important Sutra because it provided the foundations which were later developed into the idealist doctrines of the Yogacara. As in the case of the *Vimalikirti Sutra,* the Sanskrit text of this Sutra has also disappeared. It is preserved for us only in Tibetan and Chinese versions. There were five Chinese versions. Two of these are only partial translations. The other translations were done by Bodhiruci, Paramartha, and Hsüan-tsang.

The teaching of this Sutra is generally the same as in the *Wisdom Sutras;* yet this *Sutra* goes much further into the analysis of our conceptual processes and the manner in which we think and speak of the final reality. We have here, above all, an effort at clarity. This is attained most effectively in the first four chapters. These constitute a section apart that might be considered one of the clearest presentations we possess of the doctrines of nonduality, emptiness, the perfections of the Bodhisattvas, and the ways of release from involvement in the world of Samsara.

There is a clear commitment in the early part of this

Sutra to the idea of an absolute reality designated as *Para-martha, Tathata, Svabhavanihsvabhavata, Dharmanairatmya, Sunyata.* These words mean the Supreme Reality, True Nature, Absence of One's Own Nature, the Nonsubstantiality of Things, Emptiness. Also there are words such as *Daharmadhatu,* which means Fundamental Element; *Bhutakoti,* which means Absolute Point of Existence. All of these terms indicate the basic commitment of the author to a final reality that is at the opposite pole of nihilism. Defined in terms of nonduality, it is beyond both difference and identity. It is beyond all speculative comprehension, beyond words, analogies; beyond any final statement, positive or negative. The words and images that are used by man emerge from within the thinking process of man himself. There is no corresponding reality in the external world. Thus the beginnings are established for a subjective idealism such as developed in the next two centuries and finally produced the great works of Vasubandhu.

Of special importance is the section on the eighteen species of emptiness. Removal of all phenomenal reality proceeds from one point to another, from the emptiness of the elements of reality, to the emptiness of all things, to the emptiness of perception and nonperception, and so to the emptiness of the personality, to the nonexistence of the ego, to the attainment of absolute emptiness. In the end, "For him who meditates on the emptiness of all these notions there is the notion of emptiness. This itself is finally removed by the emptiness of emptiness" (*Samdhinirmocana* viii, 29/10).

Because of the directness of presentation, this Sutra might be considered one of the earliest clear syntheses that set forth most of the Mahayana doctrines. The doctrine of the Threefold Body of Buddha had not yet fully evolved, although it is presented here in the tenth chapter in a rudimentary form. The Bodhisattva doctrine, especially the doctrine on the Ten Stages of Perfection of the Bodhisattvas, is given a new precision of statement that was later taken up by the commentators of the Yogacara school.

6. The *Descent into Ceylon Sutra, Lankavatara Sutra.* This Sutra is one of the more difficult to understand and explain. It has not even the general coherence that is found in the other Mahayana Sutras. Most of these Sutras have more inspiration and insight than orderly presentation or literary form. But the *Lankavatara* consists of notes that were collected on a variety of subjects without establishing any order in subject matter or presentation. Yet it remains one of the most significant of the Sutras for its insight into the nature of the mind and its functioning. It is highly psychological and epistemological. Although it seems to be unrelated in origin to the *Samdhinirmocana Sutra,* it considers some of the same subjects. Together with that Sutra it forms the fundamental background and provides the seminal doctrines of Yogacara idealism. In its greater moments the *Lankavatara* equals in its depth of penetration any of the other great Sutras of the Mahayana. It has been especially influential on the development of Zen Buddhism because of its teaching on sudden enlightenment.

This Sutra was written in the late second or possibly the early third century. It could not have been earlier because of its dependence on the *Wisdom Sutras.* Certainly available by the mid-third century, it was used by the later Mahayana masters. It was translated into Chinese by four different translators between A.D. 420 and A.D. 704. Three of these translations are still in existence, those by Gunabhadra, Bodhiruci, and Sikshananda. The first translation by Dharmaraksha has been lost. Fortunately the Sanskrit text of this Sutra still exists. Although this Sutra has been of great importance in the development of the Mahayana tradition, it has been little studied in modern times by Western scholars. There is a translation into English by Daisetz Suzuki and a corresponding volume of studies concerning the doctrines taught in the *Lankavatara* by the same author.

The doctrine of the *Lankavatara* is given in the form of answers to 108 questions proposed to Buddha by Mahamati. These range from questions on the highest doctrines of Buddhism to questions concerning trees and mountains and the capturing of elephants. The most significant questions are those concerning the mind, for the doctrine of mind-only is the central teaching of the Sutra. There is also a first formulation of the important doctrine of later Buddhism concerning the inner consciousness of the mind which brings forth, at their proper time, the various ideas that present themselves in the mind. These ideas are not awakened in response to external stimulation; they are rather the causes for the appearance of the external world. This, in reality, is only the illusion that results from our lack of awareness that all things are mind-only. Awareness that all things are only mind is attained by a profound conversion process in the mind that enables it to become aware that its own functioning produces what seems to be the external world.

However, Mahamati, I am neither for permanency nor for impermanency. Why? For these reasons: external objects are not admitted; the triple world is taught as not being anything else but the mind itself; multiplicities of external existences are not accepted; there is no rising of the elements, nor their disappearance, nor their continuation, nor their differentiation; there are no such things as the elements primary and secondary; because of discrimination there evolve the dualistic indications of perceived and perceiving; when it is recognized that because of discrimination there is a duality, the discussion concerning the existence and nonexistence of the external world ceases because mind-only is understood. . . . According to the Buddha there is nothing in the world but the mind itself, and all that is of duality has its rise from the mind and is seen as perceived and perceiving; an ego-soul and what belongs to it—they exist not (*Lankavatara* 180–181).

This doctrine of conversion or turning back is one of the most significant elements in the *Lankavatara Sutra*. It indicates a profound change whereby the entire process of experiencing reality is suddenly altered. Everything is shifted from an objective focus to a subjective focus. The mind is suddenly aware of itself, its operations, its fundamental identity with all reality. This produces a completely new attitude that is one of the sources of the unique subjective idealism evolved in the works of Asanga and Vasubandhu, in the fifth century. It is among the most permanent and fruitful of all the discoveries made in the Mahayana tradition.

7. The *Golden Splendour Sutra, Suvarnaprabhasa*. This Sutra of twenty-one chapters in prose and verse belongs among the Sutras that have more popular than intellectual appeal. In this work special emphasis is placed on the merit of hearing it read and of showing special honour to the work itself, as in the *Lotus Sutra,* which also insists on the special, even magical value of hearing the Sutra recited. Again this is a Sutra of great popularity in the East Asian world because of its teaching concerning the blessings bestowed upon the rulers of countries that honour this Sutra and the examples of the kings discussed in it.

The principal doctrine here presented is that of the eternal existence of the Buddha. This subject, treated in the fifteenth chapter of the *Lotus Sutra,* is given detailed development in the second chapter of the *Golden Splendour Sutra.* There is also the same doctrine concerning the apparent passing of Buddha into Nirvana, which was not a real passing away but only an event in the life of the Buddha to lead those unable to desire Buddhahood at least to the desire of Nirvana.

The other principal doctrine of this Sutra is the doctrine of the emptiness of all things. Because of its insistence on the use of spells, this Sutra is very similar to the Tantric writings.

8. The *Land of Bliss Sutra, Sukhivativyuha.* This work is at the centre of the devotional tradition of Mahayana Buddhism. Of all the major Sutras it has the least intellectual depth. Yet it supplied the tremendous need experienced by the less educated peasant and working classes of the Asian world. If they could not respond to the high intellectualism of the *Wisdom Sutras,* nor to the call to Buddhahood announced in the *Lotus Sutra,* they could respond to the promise of a land of bliss that awaited them in another world. In this Sutra they received an apocalyptic vision of that land in all its splendour. At the centre of this land is the Buddha:

> The Lord of vast light, incomparable and infinite, has illumined all Buddha countries in all the quarters, he has quieted all passions, all sins and errors, he has quenched the fire in the realm of hell. . . . The splendour of sun and moon does not shine in heaven, nor the fiery splendour of the maze of jewels of the gods; the Lord overcomes all splendour, he, the bright one, who has performed his former discipline.
>
> He is the best of men, the treasure of all who suffer; there is no one like him in all the quarters. Having completed a hundred thousand good works, he, in his assembly, raised the lion-voice of Buddha (*Sukhivativyuha* ix, 5–8).

Those who enter this joyful land experience the removal of all evil and the fullness of all that is good.

> O, Ananda, there is nowhere in that Land of Bliss any sound of sin, obstacle, misfortune, distress, and destruction; there is nowhere any sound of pain, even the perception of sound that is neither pain nor pleasure is not there, O Ananda, that world is called Land of Bliss, shortly, but not in full. For, O Ananda, the whole kalpa would come to an end, while the different causes of the pleasure of the world Sukhavati are being praised, and even then the end of those causes of happiness could not be reached.
>
> O Ananda, the beings, who have been and will be born

in that world Sukhavati, will be endowed with such colour, strength, vigour, height and breadth, dominion, accumulation of virtue; with such enjoyments of dress, ornaments, gardens, palaces, and pavilions; and such enjoyments of touch, taste, smell, and sound; in fact with all enjoyments and pleasures, exactly like the Paranirmitavasavartin gods. . . .

And again, O Ananda, in that world Sukhavati, when the time of forenoon has come, the winds, greatly agitated, blow everywhere in the four quarters. They shake and sway many beautiful, graceful, and many-coloured stalks of the gem trees, which are perfumed with sweet heavenly scents, so that many hundred beautiful flowers of delightful scent fall upon the great earth, which is all full of jewels. With these flowers that Buddha country is adorned on every side seven fathoms deep. As a clever man might spread out a flower-bed on the earth and make it even with both his hands, beautiful and charming, even so with those flowers of various scents and colours that Buddha country is shining on every side seven fathoms deep (*Sukhivativyuha* xviii, xix, xxi).

This that is so radiant and lovely is obtained, not by learned studies or even by great ascetic practises. It is attained by faith in the grace of the Buddha Amitabha. "See O Ajita, what easy gains are gained by those beings who will hear the name of the Tathagata Amitabha, holy and fully enlightened. Nor will those beings be of little faith who obtain at least one joyful thought of that Tathagata and of this treatise of the Law" (*Sukhivativyuha* xliii). That all beings would have easy access to this blissful country had been the prayer of the Buddha Amitayu: "This prayer was mine formerly, that beings having in any way whatever heard my name should forever go to my country. And this my excellent prayer has been fulfilled, and beings quickly come here from many worlds into my presence, never return from here, not even for one birth" (*Sukhivativyuha* xxxi, 17–18).

Besides this longer *Sutra of the Land of Bliss* there is another shorter version which has an even greater emphasis on the attainment of paradise by the remembrance of the name of Buddha Amitabha.

Beings are not born into that Buddha country of the Tathagata Amitayus as a reward and result of good works performed in this present life. No, whatever son or daughter of a family shall hear the name of the blessed Amitayus, the Tathagata, and having heard it, shall keep it in mind, and with thoughts undisturbed shall keep it in mind for one, two, three, four, five, six or seven nights—when that son or daughter of a family comes to die, then Amitayus, the Tathagata, surrounded by an assembly of disciples and followed by a host of Bodhisattvas, will stand before them at their hour of death, and they will depart this life with tranquil minds. After their death they will be born in the world Sukhavati, in the Buddha country of the same Amitayus, the Tathagata (*Smaller Sukhivativyuha Sutra* x).

CHAPTER XVI

THE MAHAYANA SCHOOLS

Toward the end of the Sutra period, at the close of the second century B.C. the great Mahayana masters began to appear on the scene of Buddhist development. These men produced the first learned expositions of Mahayana doctrine. With extraordinary intelligence and depth of spiritual insight, they worked in a Buddhist tradition that was coming to a new maturity of expression. The original Buddha-vision had produced a distinctive type of intellectual inquiry associated with personal salvation. A spiritual urgency was intrinsic to the intellectual effort. This was not a philosophy that arose from curiosity concerning the make-up of the objective world; this was spiritual vision concerned with salvation from the human condition.

By the third century A.D. this effort had been in process for some seven centuries. The fruitfulness of the original vision of Buddha had proved itself in many areas of man's life. Spiritually it had enabled large numbers of people to deal with the sorrows of time in the hope of a transtemporal release from these afflictions. Emotionally it had given men serenity with a great depth of inner assurance. Artistically it had produced some of the finest artworks of the Asian world. Now in the Great Tradition of Buddhism, the Mahayana, a new surge of life was felt in all spheres of Buddhist activity. The supreme achievement at this moment was the creation of a new intellectual tradition. Yet the spiritual and artistic success of Buddhism at this time has been appreciated by the Western world much more than the intellectual accomplishment. To appreciate the latter requires a linguistic training combined with spiritual and intellectual capacities that few western scholars have yet attained. The entire effort of the Mahayana was to effect a spiritual purification of the mind from all its rational and conceptual processes, to obtain release from the imprisonment that the mind imposes on itself—unless by an inner discipline it keeps itself above and free from the limitations that are the immediate result of its own functioning. The most significant aspect of man's intellectual life is this capacity to go beyond all that he thinks and expresses. The work of the Mahayana is not exactly to produce this nonconceptual experience; it is rather to establish the conditions in which this experience can take place.

Intellectually the earlier Buddhism, the Hinayana, had made its final contribution in the works known as *Abhidharma*. Of a highly psychological nature, these efforts sought a systematic classification of the elements of the physical and psychological worlds. They were not reasoned treatises. In themselves they provided no great depth of insight. They even tended to negate and to obstruct the very insight that Buddha had provided. But at least they provided terms and classifications of psychic and physical phenomena that could be used when the time came for a more metaphysical and more spiritual type of intellectual activity such as that undertaken by the Mahayana scholars.

The new Mahayana scriptures represent the moment when Buddhist thinkers realized the obstructive element in the *Abhidharma* literature. A thought dialectic was in process. Looking back from the present, it seems that the *Abhidharma* stage was necessary, that these terms and classifications had first to be set forth and then used against themselves in a critical type of analysis. The central feature of the Hinayana world-view had been its commitment to the real existence of dharmas. These dharmas are the basic elements of reality with only momentary existence that integrate and disintegrate into those objects and activities that constitute the world about us. The Hinayana schools discussed and disagreed constantly over these dharmas, the period of their endurance, the process by which they came into and passed out of existence; but there was general agreement on two propositions: the dharmas were real, they were transitory.

Reacting against this commitment to the reality of dharmas, the earliest Mahayana Sutras, the *Perfection of Wisdom Sutras,* established as their central doctrine *sunyata,* emptiness, the nonexistence of dharmas. These dharmas as described in the *Heart Sutra* are *svabhavasunya,* "empty in their own being." Dharmas neither come into existence nor pass out of existence. They are illusory as a dream or a mirage. Awareness of this fact constitutes the central element in a truly liberating wisdom. This doctrine of sunyata produced great intellectual excitement among the early Mahayana writers. They endlessly repeated their assertions concerning the emptiness of dharmas. Finally they had seen through the confining commitment to an objective world.

This revolution in Buddhist thought was a second turning of the wheel of Buddhist doctrine. Whereas Buddha had the original experience of the disintegration of things, of the insubstantial nature of the world, this new vision was a more mature statement of this same doctrine. The Mahayana was both an evolution and a return, with a deepened awareness of the original intuitions of Buddha. Within this new tradition, two tendencies can be discerned from the beginning. First there was the negative critique of the *Abhidharma* to establish the doctrine of sunyata. The other tendency, with greater psychological interest, insisted that this approach was too negative, that apparent phenomena themselves required some basis and that this was to be found in the doctrine that only consciousness existed. Salvation was attained by returning the mind to its pure state. The world of particularity was a defilement of the original pure state. Contained in the depth of this ultimate reality of consciousness were all the ideas and imaginings that we associate with the external world. They exist, as it were, in a storehouse consciousness. Self-evoked, they produce the unending series of images that to unreflexive man constitute the surrounding world.

In both these traditions a number of outstanding figures arose who became the founders and great masters of the Mahayana schools. They were followed by the scholar-monks who produced a new type of scholasticism. Here Buddhism found its final spiritual-intellectual expression in India. All of this took place in the seven centuries between the late second century and the early ninth century A.D.

The tradition that gave a negative critique of the *Abhidharma* doctrines, in order to establish the doctrine of sunyata only, came to be known as the Madhyamika or Middle Way School. Denying both existence and nonexistence it proposed a very strict doctrine of sunyata only. The founder and greatest master of this school was Nagarjuna. This writer may well be the most influential single thinker known to the Asian world. The teaching he communicated to the Asian world is the basic philosophy of Mahayana Buddhism. It had great influence on the later development of the Yogacara or idealist school of Mahayana Buddhism. Through Gaudapada it directly influenced the highest intellectual attainment of Hinduism, the Advaita Vedanta of Sankara. It was a strong element in the rise of Zen Buddhism. It comes closest to what Westerners generally think of as "Oriental" thought. It is this philosophy that is fundamental to much of the art and poetry of China and Japan.

Of Nagarjuna we know little with certainty. Evidently he came from south India and spent a good part of his life there. Legend says that he taught at the great Buddhist centre of Nalanda, but there is no way of substantiating this story. India's thinkers had little use for biographical details of the men who produced their intellectual or artistic traditions. The Chinese and Tibetans, however, could not do without such details. But even they in their legends of Nagarjuna tell us little of his life except that he lived and worked much of his life in the coastal regions of south India.

In the Chinese canon some twenty-four works are ascribed to Nagarjuna. In the Tibetan list six major works are assigned to Nagarjuna. It seems clear that a number of works were attributed to him that are not truly authentic. Yet two of his works should be mentioned here. The first is the *Mulamadhyamakakarika,* the other is the *Mahaprajnaparamita Shastra.* This latter work is not certainly by Nagarjuna. Yet it does give expression to his basic ideas and should be studied in connection with his thought.

The other work, the *Mulamadhyamakakarika,* is certainly by Nagarjuna and can be considered the single most important work in the Madhyamika tradition. It is as important for Mahayana Buddhism as the *Brahma Sutra* is for the Vedanta tradition of Hinduism. All the major figures in the Madhyamika tradition wrote commentaries on this Shastra. There are eight principal commentaries. The first is by Nagarjuna himself. The others are by Arya Deva, Buddhapalita, Bhavaviveka, Sthiramati, Candrakirti, Sarman, and Gunasri. Of these, only that of Candrakirti survives in the original Sanskrit. The others survive in Chinese and/or Tibetan translation.

The *Madhyamika Shastra* has a text of 27 chapters, with a total of 448 verses. The doctrine proposed is that things exist in appearance only. Sunyata is not separate from but identical with the apparent world. While it is not difficult to understand the critique whereby appearances are negated in favour of a final emptiness as the absolute beyond appearance, it is difficult to follow Nagarjuna in his next step, which is to identify the two. Nirvana and Samsara, the transphenomenal sunyata and the unreal empirical world, are one and the same thing. This is insisted on absolutely in the *Karikas*. The first verse of the *Karikas* begins with the powerful statement: "Neither out of itself, nor out of another, nor out of both, nor out of any cause does there arise any being whatsoever, of any kind, in any place" (Nagarjuna, *Karikas*, v. 1). This statement and the explanation given in the verses that follow established a new intellectual position in Buddhism.

This new position was carried on to more complete expression by Arya Deva, the first and most faithful disciple of Nagarjuna. Arya Deva lived in the third century A.D. While Nagarjuna was completely occupied with his opposition to the realism of the *Abhidharma,* Arya Deva sought to establish the new tradition by carrying on a polemic against the Hindu philosophical schools, the Samkhya and the Vaisesika. The work that expresses the substance of his thought is the *Catuh Sataka,* The Four Hundred Verses. These verses are strictly in the pattern of Nagarjuna's thought. They provide an enlargement but are without any new or unique doctrinal development. Yet because of its detailed exposition of the basic thought of the Madhyamika, the *Catuh Sataka* has a place in this thought tradition next to the *Karikas* of Nagarjuna. A number of commentaries on this work appeared in Sanskrit. But the original and the commentaries have been lost in their Sanskrit, text and survive only in translation, Chinese and/or Tibetan.

After Arya Deva came two outstanding scholars in the Madhyamika tradition who fixed the two basic trends within this school, Buddhapalita and Bhavaviveka. Both wrote commentaries on the *Karikas* of Nagarjuna. Both carried on discussion with the Hindu thinkers of the period, especially with the Samkhya and Vaisesika philosophers. Yet they had different interpretations of the final message of the Madhyamika.

Buddhapalita left a decisive impression on the Madhyamika school through his teaching that no positive arguments could be brought forth in support of the sunyata doctrine of Nagarjuna. The only sound process of reasoning on this subject was that whereby opposed doctrines were shown to be absurd. The final conclusion concerning our contact with a so-called outer world is through the use of names that are simply empty expressions. To sustain this negative critique was a difficult thing, but it was achieved with special brilliance by Buddhapalita.

Yet his arguments did not satisfy his successor, Bhavaviveka, who lived also in the beginning of the fifth century. Bhavaviveka could not accept the basic position of his predecessors that the final wisdom was a negative critique and rejection of all philosophical positions without positive arguments for any doctrinal affirmations. The undeviating process of mental purification set forth by Buddhapalita was explicitly rejected by Bhavaviveka. His arguments were set forth in his commentary on the *Karikas* of Nagarjuna and also in his works entitled *Madhyamakartha Sangraha, Madhyamakavatara-Pradipa,* and *Madhyamaka Pratitya Samutpada.* Much of his writing in these works is directed against the representatives of the Yogacara tradition. Yet in his fundamental position he accepted much more of the Yogacara thought than any other thinker of the early Madhyamika tradition. Although less influential than Buddhapalita, Bhavaviveka was richer in the range and complexity of his thought. In the midst of this complexity he insisted on the "Middle Way," which was the original position of Buddha and the basic claim of the Madhyamika. With Buddhapalita this "Middle Way" tended too much towards the direction of nonexistence. Bhavaviveka recalled the words of Buddha to Kasyapa. "Eternal is one extreme, noneternal is the other extreme. What lies between in the middle of both, that is formless, beyond designation, without form, without manifestation, without knowledge and without qualification. That is what is meant by the Middle Way, the true consideration of the nature of all phenomena." He also quotes Buddha to the effect that "Knowledge and ignorance is not twofold and constitutes no duality." Correct knowledge of these, that is what it meant by the Middle Way.

This advance of Bhavaviveka in the direction of a more comprehensive doctrine led to the response of Candrakirti at the end of the sixth century. Candrakirti was taught by Kamalabuddhi, who in turn had studied under Buddhapalita and Bhavaviveka. Candrakirti wrote a number of works: The *Madhyamakavatara,* an independent work of his own and commentaries on Nagarjuna's works, *Sunyata Saptati* and *Yukti Sastika.* He also wrote a commentary on the *Catuh Sataka* of Arya Deva. His greatest work, however, the one that established Candrakirti as the most decisive influence in the later history of Madhyamika thought, is the *Prasannapada,* a commentary on Nagarjuna's *Karikas.* This work is a study of extraordinary clarity that supports the strict interpretation of Nagarjuna given by Buddhapalita. It was done so well that it has ever since been almost inseparable from the masterful work of Nagarjuna. Nagarjuna is studied as much through the work of Candrakirti as he is directly in his own work. This brought about an eclipse in the significance of the work of Bhavaviveka. While it did strengthen the absolute quality of the negative critical method of the Madhyamika, it also strengthened the division between the Madhyamika and the Yogacara.

In explaining the opening verses of the *Madhyamakakarika,* Candrakirti insists on the absurdity of something rising out of itself as a cause, for in this instance the existing being would be negating itself. If something arose out of it, then either it did not exist in the first place, or if it did exist then nothing could arise out of it, for it would already be existing and could not arise anew. Then in explaining that the Madhyamika defender cannot be accused of error he insists on the fact that the Madhyamika makes no assertion about anything and comes to no conclusion. Therefore there is no occasion for error. In support of this position he quotes the

Catuh Sataka of Arya Deva (xvi, v. 25): "To contradict him who in no way makes any assertion, whether concerning being, nonbeing, or being and nonbeing at the same time, is not possible on any occasion." Candrakirti further maintains: "Since Madhyamika sets forth no independent conclusion, what has it to do with any independent assertion?" It would be difficult to imagine a more consistent process of argument than that set forth by Candrakirti. It is another instance of the capacity of the Indian mind to establish a direction of thought and then to pursue it with undeviating insistence to its most extreme conclusion. This power of exhausting the possibilities of distinctive thought trends brings forth a metaphysical depth of analysis that remains difficult for those outside the tradition to appreciate.

While the Madhyamika tradition was bringing forth such an impressive series of scholars, another tradition within the Mahayana, the Yogacara or idealist tradition, was also establishing itself as a spiritual-intellectual tradition of equal distinction. This Yogacara tradition, although firmly based on the *Perfection of Wisdom Sutras* and strongly influenced by the sunyata doctrine of the Madhyamika, was dominated by the tradition of the *Lankavatara* and the *Samdhinirmocana Sutras*. The Yogacara agreed with the Madhyamika that the outer world was only apparent, not real. But the Yogacara considered that behind this world of appearance was a thought process. At times there are indications that the Yogacara accepted the real existence of the mind itself as a substantial reality. Yet the more precise position of the Yogacara school is that there is neither a substantial objective world nor a substantial subjective world, but only a conscious activity. This activity is without subjective support or objective reference. This process itself is real. All else is unreal. The first really impressive statement of the Yogacara idealism is contained in the *Samdhinirmocana,* the *Explanation of Mysteries Sutra.*

vi. 3. Things have a threefold character. What are these three? The imaginary character, the dependent character, and the absolute character.

4. What is the imaginary character? These are the names, the conventions that attribute to things a proper nature, and the specifications that allow us to refer to them in our current speech.

5. What is the dependent aspect? It is the production of things through their causes, which is expressed by saying, "This being so, that is" or "This coming into being, that comes into being." So it is said, "Things acting do so by reason of ignorance" and "This is the origin of this entire mass of suffering."

6. What is the absolute character? It is the true nature of things, the discovery by the Bodhisattvas of this true nature by reason of their effort and their keen reflection; and finally the attaining of supreme enlightenment due to practise of this discovery.

7. The imaginary character is like the false vision that affects a man with an eye ailment. The dependent character is like the images that appear to a person with an eye ailment, bits of hair, flies, grains of sesame; objects blue, yellow, red, or white. The absolute character is like the true objects, the proper objects of the eye when a man has his eyes perfectly clear and when the eye ailment has disappeared.

8. It is just as in the case of transparent crystal. In contact with blue, it takes on the appearance of sapphire, genuine or artificial. When the crystal is wrongly taken for sapphire it deceives everyone. In contact with red, green, or yellow, the crystal takes on the appearance of a ruby, emerald, or gold. When mistaken for a jewel of this kind, it deceives everyone.

9. The implications of current language, essentially a work of imagination affecting the dependent character of things, can be compared to the presence of colours that effect transparent crystal. Falsely to attribute to the dependent character the imaginative character is equivalent to falsely attributing the nature of sapphire,

ruby, emerald, or gold to transparent crystal. The dependent character can be compared to the transparent crystal. Finally the absolute character is the nonreality, the perpetual nonexistence of the imaginary character attributed to the dependent character. Just as the absolute character of the crystal is the nonreality, the enduring nonexistence of the characters of sapphire and the other jewels attributed to the crystal.

10. The imaginary characters rest on the names attached to ideas. The dependent character rests on the attribution of imaginary character to dependent character. The absolute character rests on the nonattribution of imaginary characters to dependent characters.

11. The Bodhisattva who knows imaginary characters falsely attributed to the dependent character of things, knows things as simply without character. Those who know exactly the dependent character, know exactly the things that stain. Those who know exactly the absolute character, know exactly the means of purification (*Samdhinirmocana Sutra* vi, 3–11).

These ideas were taken up by the first of the Yogacara masters, known to us by name Maitreyanatha. This scholar is the least known to us by any biographical details of his life. His real existence as anything more than a name has been questioned. In the attribution of works to their authors there is a tendency to attribute works with little distinction to Maitreyanatha and Asanga, who was the successor of Maitreyanatha. Yet there is a growing conviction that such a person as Maitreyanatha did exist and that he is the author of the *Abhisamayalamkarah*, the *Mahayanasutralamkarah*, and the *Madhyantavibhagah*. In these works he produced the first extensive scholastic literature of the Yogacara.

Some idea of the thought of Maitreyanatha can be obtained from this passage of the *Mahayanasutralamkarah:*

As in a properly executed painting there are in reality no heights or depths, although it seems so, so there is no duality whatsoever in our unreal conception, though it seems to be.

As in disturbed and then calmed waters, clarity is not derived from anywhere but only by the removal of the obstructing matter, this same rule is valid also for the purification of the mind. The meaning is simply that the mind is of its nature clear. Only through outer defects is it disturbed. Outside of the mind resting on the essence of reality there is no other mind from which clarity could be obtained (*Mahayanasutralamkarah* xiii, 17–19).

After Maitreyanatha came Asanga in the mid-fourth century A.D. He lived originally in the extreme northwest of India. The most important of his works are the *Abhidharmasamuccayah* and the *Mahayanasamgrahah*. This latter work, whose title might be translated as *Synthesis of Mahayana,* is one of the most successful syntheses of Mahayana thought. It has a philosophical depth that makes it of special interest to all who are interested in the intellectual structure of Mahayana Buddhism. In this work he brought over into the Mahayana and transformed considerably the terminology of the Hinayana *Abhidharma*. This already had a strong psychological emphasis that made it especially suited to the Yogacara tradition. To the earlier examples of the crystal and the picture, Asanga adds and explains the analogy of the mental operations with the dream.

In dream there appear, although no object is present and only the thought process is real, the images of many objects, of form, colour, sound, taste, feeling, images of a house, a forest, a landscape, a mountain, and yet no object is really present. On the basis of this example we can recognize that in every case the knowing process alone is real. This is even more clear if we consider the unreal appearances of magic, mirage and optical illusion. If the question is asked why it is that we do not recognize in a dream that the dream is unreal and that knowledge alone is real, the answer is that only those know who are awakened to the awareness of reality. Just as in dream this awareness does not exist, but only with those who are awake, so it is not given to those who are not awakened to the true reality in a final sense, although it is given to such as attain a real understanding of truth (*Mahayanasamgraha* ii, 6–7).

Asanga developed a very complex manner of explaining just how the ideation process takes place, what stirs it to action, and how it is gradually purified until it attains a final awareness of itself and escapes the illusions that are attached to its activities. First there is the storehouse consciousness, or the ideation store, in which the seeds of these imaginations are contained. These seeds produce manifestations which in turn "perfume" or "saturate" the ideation store to produce other seeds and other manifestations. The original seeds exist from an infinite period of the past until the present. There was no question of identifying the beginning of things in the Indian mind. When finally there is no grasping of any objective reality, then the purification is attained. The mind attains a quiescence in itself according to the stages of concentration established in the Buddhist tradition from the beginning.

After Asanga came the renowned master Vasubandhu. He came from the same region as Asanga, from the northwest of India, Gandhara. A large number of commentaries are attributed to him. Also a series of original treatises. To him is attributed the great synthesis of the Sarvastivada school known as the *Abhidharmakosa*. It may well be that this work was done by a different Vasubandhu than the one known for his commentaries in the Yogacara tradition. It may also be that this synthesis of a Hinayana school was a production of the same person at an earlier stage of his life and that he then entered into another tradition and produced works of a new order. Indeed his familiarity with the other schools of Hinayana thought may well have been of advantage to him as a Mahayana thinker. Vasubandhu was a younger brother of Asanga. Both seem to have been connected with Hinayana schools before dedicating their efforts to the exposition of Yogacara doctrines. But though Vasubandhu did an exceptional amount of work in commentary form, the greatest of his Yogacara works are the two short treatises known as *Vijnaptimatratasiddi; Vimsatika* and *Vijnaptimatratasiddh Trimsika.* These titles may be translated as *The Treatise on Ideation Only in Twenty Stanzas* and *The Treatise on Ideation Only in Thirty Stanzas.* A long list of commentaries were written on these two works in the later period of the Yogacara school. Vasubandhu was a scholar in the strict sense of the word. He had much less concern with the salvation problem, with the stages of spiritual perfection, than Asanga or most of the other Mahayana writers.

Throughout the course of Indian thought there is constant reference to the dream experience. So with Vasubandhu the dream experience is again used to speak of the knowledge that we have in our world of particularity and which is dissolved when we awaken in a higher degree of consciousness. But in his work, *Vimsatika* (Ch. xvii), Vasubandhu presses the question further by inquiring how there is an apparent influence of one person on another, since the entire ideation process is so individual and so interior, as in the case of a dream. The answer is that the ideation process in one living being occasions a similar ideation process in the conscious awareness of another living being. These determine each other by a reciprocal influence without there being any real exterior objects.

After Vasubandhu came several scholars who attained renown for their commentaries and for their work as teachers, some of them at the famous university at Nalanda. There was, first of all, Dharmapala, an opponent of Bhavaviveka. Dharmapala was the most famous representative of the Yogacara idealism at Nalanda. He was succeeded by Silabhadra, the teacher of Hsüan-tsang, the Chinese pilgrim-scholar, during five years of Hsüan-tsang's stay at Nalanda. It was the tradition of Silabhadra that was carried to China and there gave rise to the ideation school. Then there were two other scholars of distinction, Gunamati and Sthiramati, both of whom were strongly influenced by Vasubandhu.

A further distinctive development out of the Yogacara school was the development of a school of logicians that had an important influence on the development of Buddhism in India and influenced considerably the later development of Indian thought even outside of Buddhism. The most significant creators of this new science were Dinaga and Dharmakirti, both of southern India, both of Brahman descent, both followers of Vasubandhu.

The story of this school of thought and its place in the general development of Buddhism are not well known. Yet the later history of Buddhism had some of its most important representatives in this tradition. It is significant that the scientific development of logic took place in the Yogacara tradition. The problems of epistemology led gradually in this direction, for Buddhist argumentation became ultrarefined during the fifth and sixth centuries. This was also when the Hindu schools of thought were showing their full strength for the first time. That it was a period of endless discussion and debate, we can see from the accounts given us by the Chinese travellers. They themselves, at times, participated in these controversies.

Dinaga, who lived in the sixth century, was the most brilliant representative of this new tradition. The story of his life indicates that he was a student of Vasubandhu when the latter was an old man. Although this is founded on insufficient evidence, it is certain that Dinaga was inspired by several of the logical treatises of Vasubandhu. In his early life he wrote a summary of the great synthesis of his teacher under the title *Abhidharmakosa-marma-pradipa*. But his really great work was entitled *Pramana-samuccaya*. This was a summary and deepened interpretation of the other logical works which he had done previously.

In the second generation after Dinaga we find the other master of the science of logic, Dharmakirti. Also from the south of India, he went first to Nalanda to receive instruction from Dharmapala. Later he became a student under Isvarasena, who had studied under Dinaga. Seven of the works of Dharmakirti have come down to us. These have established themselves as the basic works of the science of logic in the Buddhist tradition and also as basic works in the broader field of Indian tradition. These works, except for the one entitled *Nyayabindu,* have been lost in their Sanskrit versions. They are all available in Tibetan translation. The greatest of his works is entitled *Pramana-vartika.*

Besides the Madhyamika, the Yogacara, and the logicians, another trend in the Buddhist Mahayana tradition that deserves attention is that found in the works of Ashvaghosa and Saramati. Of these Ashvaghosa is the earlier. He was a powerful influence in China. Neither Ashvaghosa nor Saramati were of great influence on Buddhist thought in India. Still the name of Ashvaghosa is of such distinction that it would not be proper to leave him out of any survey of Mahayana Buddhism in India.

Ashvaghosa is generally considered as the earliest of the great Mahayana teachers. He lived at the end of the second century A.D. during the reign of Kanishka. A large number of works are attributed to him. Of these the *Buddhacarita,* the *Life of Buddha,* is the best known. The first complete life of Buddha in the classical Buddhist tradition, it was written with an exalted, elaborate style that brought out the marvellous aspect of the legends that had been handed down from the beginning. This work and the *Saundarananda-Kavya* belong to the earliest period of classical Sanskrit literature. They have a vigorous style combined with a typical Indian elegance which merits recognition. Some idea of the picturesque quality of the *Buddhacarita* can be gathered from the opening description of the place of his birth:

There was a city, the dwelling-place of the great saint Kapila, having its sides surrounded by the beauty of a lofty broad table-land as by a line of clouds, and itself, with its high-soaring palaces, immersed in the sky.

By its pure and lofty system of government it stole the splendour of the clouds of Mount Kailasa, and while it bore the clouds which came to it by mistake, it fulfilled the imagination which had led them thither.

In that city, shining with the splendour of gems, darkness, like poverty, could find no place: prosperity shone resplendently, as with a smile, from the joy of dwelling with such surpassingly excellent citizens.

With its festive arbours, its arched gateways and pinnacles it was radiant with jewels in every dwelling; and unable to find any other rival in the world, it could only feel emulation with its own houses.

There the sun, even though he had retired, was unable to scorn the moon-like faces of its women which put the lotuses to shame, and as if from the access of passion, hurried towards the western ocean to enter the cooling water (*Buddhacarita* i, 2–6).

The treatise entitled the *Mahayanasraddhotpadasastra* (*The Awakening of Faith in the Mahayana*), which now exists only in a Chinese text, is attributed to Ashvaghosa. Although it may not be his work, yet it goes under his name and deserves consideration here as a contribution to the school of thought that became known as the Tathata tradition. This is a very secondary tradition in India, although later, in China, it was an influence of more extensive proportions. If this work constantly asserts that the entire phenomenal world is unreal, it does so only to assert the final reality of a metaphysical ultimate designated as *Tathata*, "Thusness." In this way *The Awakening of Faith* seems to be closer to the absolutism of the Upanishads and to the Nirguna Brahman concept of the Advaita Vedanta than to the Mahayana Buddhism of the Yogacara School with which it is frequently associated. The entire phenomenal world is considered a manifestation of this one final reality. The world of change and visible form is considered an illusion, as *maya*—to use the classical expression for the tangible world in the Vedantic tradition.

The association with the Yogacara idealism comes from the doctrine of *The Awakening of Faith* that the external world arises from within the human mind. In this *The Awakening of Faith* is entirely different from the Vedantic explanation of the apparent but unreal world. Vedanta explains the apparent world by its relationship with Brahman in the form of Isvara, the Lord, who by his power produces the appearances that we consider as the real world about us. *The Awakening of Faith* asserts that all differences of things arise from the imperfect notions of the mind: "As reflections in a mirror; when the mind acts, then the different things arise; when the mind ceases its activity, then the different things cease to be."

The ideal is to return to the original condition of the mind, which is a condition of purity. This had great appeal to the Chinese because of their long tradition that wisdom in its perfection involved a return of man to his original nature. A similar ideal had been set forth by Mencius in the fourth century B.C. On the basis of this native tradition and a corresponding tradition derived from the famous work of Lao Tzu, the Chinese had already developed a process of cultivating the original mind. Now in returning to this tradition from within Buddhism they could associate the two traditions in a more complete spirituality than that contained merely within their own traditions.

There was also the appeal of a final reality that was quite close to their own idea of the *Tao,* a supreme reality beyond all form and designation. This established a direct means of understanding the Tathata. Both are concerned with a formless presence in the world of form. Yet here again the distinctive element in the tradition of Buddhist idealism asserted itself, for the dynamic of the Tao is in the cosmic order whereas the dynamic of the Tathata concept is in the mind; indeed it is the mind.

Another exposition of the basic doctrine of *The Awakening of Faith* is found in the third century writer Saramati. Coming from central India, he arrived on the scene just as the *Wisdom Sutras* were attaining their highest development in the work of Nagarjuna. He established his doctrine in direct opposition to the doctrine of sunyata as the final expression of human wisdom. This negative process of thought sponsored by the Madhyamika evoked in Saramati the assertion of a supreme reality with positive attributes. However negative be the expression of man's critique of the phenomenal world, there was a need to express the reality of the transphenomenal world in terms of real being. He established "Thusness" as the supreme designation. But along with this term he used such terms such as Supreme Reality, *Paramarthadhatuh;* Buddha Reality, *Buddhadhatuh;* and the Reality of Element, *Dharmadhatuh.* As Supreme Being the Tathata is also the Body of Supreme Truth, *Paramarthakayah.* As the Body of the Law the Tathata is the *Dharmakayah.* As the Reality of the World he is *Rupakayah.* All reality in its total form constitutes the Buddha reality in its completeness. These are the doctrines contained in Saramati's most significant work, the *Ratnagotravibhagah.*

There remain a number of significant writers who should be mentioned before leaving this section on the great masters and scholars of the Mahayana.

First there is Santi Deva, who lived in the late seventh century A.D. One of the most unique of all Buddhist writers, he is known for the great compassion that is expressed in his works, particularly in his poetry. This rises at times to superb heights. He worked in the tradition of Nagarjuna. But unlike Nagarjuna he was more concerned with the spiritual-salvation problem of a suffering world than with an intellectual critique of proposed explanations of reality. This does not mean that he was not himself a scholar of significant proportions. Indeed his work, *Siksa-samuccaya*, is a compendium of Mahayana doctrines of the greatest importance. Because it is constructed with excerpts from the most basic Sutras of the Mahayana it is doubly important, for it contains quotations from many works that have been either lost completely or lost in their Sanskrit texts. These quotations are contained in twenty-seven headings. Here, as in his other work, it is clear that his central preoccupation is to outline the Mahayana path of purification.

The other work of Santi Deva, the *Bodhicaryavatara*, is a long but extremely successful poem of Buddhist devotion. It expresses as no other work in Buddhist literature, perhaps as no other work in Asian literature, the profound longing within man for not only his own salvation but also the salvation of all mankind. This is the final reach of Buddhist compassion. It is very striking that this should be attained out of the Madhyamika tradition just after the logical works of Dinaga and Dharmakirti had been set forth in the Yogacara tradition. We can obtain some idea of his devotion to a suffering world from the following passage:

> May I be a balm to the sick, their healer and servitor, until sickness come never again; may I quench with rains of food and drink the anguish of hunger and thirst; may I be in the famine of the age's end their drink and meat; may I become an unfailing store for the poor, and serve them with manifold things for their need. My own being and my pleasures, all my righteousness in the past, present, and future I surrender indifferently, that all creatures may win to their end. The Stillness lies in surrender of all things, and my spirit is fain for the Stillness; if I must surrender all, it is best to give it for fellow-creatures. . . . I would be a protector of the unprotected, a guide of wayfarers, a ship, a dyke, and a bridge for them who seek the further Shore; a lamp for them who need a lamp, a bed for them who need a bed, a slave for all beings who need a slave. I would be a magic gem, a lucky jar, a spell of power, a sovereign balm, a wish-

ing-tree, a cow of plenty, for embodied beings. As the earth and other elements are for the manifold service of the countless creatures dwelling in the whole of space, so may I in various wise support the whole sphere of life lodged in space, until all be at peace (*Path of Light,* pp. 41–42).

After such high spiritual feeling we return to the more intellectual problems of Mahayana Buddhism and to the final developments of the Madhyamika tradition as these are represented by Santirakshita and Kamalasila. These two men, who lived at the end of the eighth century, brought Buddhism to Tibet and established there the Madhyamika tradition. Tibetan enthusiasm for Buddhism was at its peak for several centuries after this introduction. A vast translation program was begun. Texts were transcribed, particularly the texts of the Madhyamika tradition, which have since been lost in the original Sanskrit and which now must be studied in Tibetan translation.

If this expansion of Buddhism was one of the significant aspects of the work of Santirakshita and Kamalasila there are also other significant contributions that they have made to Buddhist tradition. Most important is their share in the final trend of the Madhyamika tradition towards a synthesis with the Yogacara. This was manifested first by Santirakshita and then by his student, Kamalasila. The most important works of Santirakshita are the *Tattvasangraha* and the *Madhyamikalankara.* In these works we can see the similarity with the Yogacara school in his explanation of the empirical world in its relationship to the inner consciousness. But we can also see the commitment to the sunyata concept in explaining the mind and consciousness itself. Thus there is a refusal to recognize any final reality to the ideation process. This is what keeps Santirakshita within the Madhyamika tradition.

Kamalasila is known for his work *Madhyamikaloka,* a work that carries the same essential doctrine as the works of his teacher, Santirakshita.

With these two, the work of the great teachers and scholars of the Mahayana came to an end in India. It had been a long and brilliant tradition which henceforth would live in other lands rather than in the land of its birth. Yet it remains one of the most fruitful periods in man's inquiry into the world before him and into the functioning of his own mind.

PART III

THE EXPANSION OF BUDDHISM

CHAPTER XVII

BUDDHISM IN ASIA

Despite this amazing spiritual and intellectual development, Buddhism had declined and almost disappeared in India by the year A.D. 1000. Within a few more centuries it would be practically unknown within the borders of the Indian subcontinent. But long prior to this time Buddhism had become a spiritual tradition known to most of the peoples of the Far Asian region of the world. Later it would be communicated even to the Mongols of central Asia. In the full geographical extent of its influences Buddhism has affected the geographical region that lies between Ceylon, India, and Afghanistan in the southwest and Korea and Japan in the northeast, between Mongolia in the northwest and Indonesia in the southeast. This is one of the most complex areas of the world as regards both the land and the peoples that dwell there. Here we find the world's greatest highlands in Tibet, the desert regions of the Takla Makan and the Gobi; the mountains, rivers, and coastal plains of China; the volcanic islands of Japan; the jungles of southeast Asia. The peoples who live in this region are as diverse as the Caucasian and non-Caucasian types of India, the Mongolian, the Chinese, Uigur Turks, Manchu, Korean, Japanese, Malay, Tibeto-Burmese, Thai, and Singhalese, and a great number of other peoples. The linguistic diversity corresponds with this ethnic diversity. This region contains at least half of the population of the world.

Although this region does not constitute the whole of

Asia, which also includes Siberian Asia, other portions of central Asia, and the whole of southwest Asia, this is the part of Asia that in classical times was least touched by Western civilization, the Asia that most deserves the name as this is used in opposition to the Western and European world.

This is the Asia not only of Buddhism but also of Hinduism, Confucianism, Taoism, Shinto, Shamanism, Animism, and of numerous local religious cults. Two cultures within this region, the Hindu culture of India and the Confucian culture of China, are among the most monumental and most different on the surface of the earth. Each of these many traditions of Asia has its area of determination of human life in its various aspects. Yet it can be said that there have been no common institutions and no cultural bonds extending over this entire area except those formed by Buddhism. This spiritual tradition has provided this region with a multinational and multicultural community. Only Buddhism has enabled the region to experience itself as a cultural community. To study this area as a cultural region is to study Buddhism. To study Buddhism in its full range of expression is to study this region. This cultural extension of Buddhism is the first dimension that should be understood by anyone who wishes to measure the cultural significance of Buddhism.

From its very beginning Buddhism has shown an exceptional capacity to communicate itself to men of diverse conditions of race, language, class, and culture. This does not mean that in this cultural area the different peoples have all responded to Buddhism in precisely the same way or that the cultural diversity of the region has been eliminated. It does mean that in addition to the native cultural elements throughout this region there has been added a spiritual tradition that is transcultural and multicultural in its expression. As a transcultural spiritual tradition Buddhism has given to the entire region certain spiritual and cultural developments which are common throughout or at least throughout its major portion. As a multicultural tradition Buddhism has been extensively differentiated by this contact with a variety of cultural traditions.

Here we might note the extent to which Buddhism produced a personal intercultural communication throughout this region. There are no individuals who travelled the whole area, but within the Buddhist tradition there has been an extensive communication between peoples of different cultures and different languages. The learned personalities who travelled throughout this region until the end of the fifteenth century were mostly Buddhists who sought to propagate Buddhist doctrine, to visit the holy lands and temples and shrines of Buddhism, or to undertake advanced study under Buddhist masters in some foreign land. Indians went abroad in large numbers during the first thousand years of the Christian era when Buddhism was communicated to the other countries within this area. Monks from India went to Ceylon and Burma in the pre-Christian period; then to central Asia and China, to Indonesia, Cambodia, Thailand, and Vietnam. The last of the great Indian missionary scholars, Asita, went to Tibet in the eleventh century.

Monks from China went to the small Buddhist kingdoms of central Asia, then on to India to learn, obtain the sacred writings, and visit the holy places of Buddhism. Some of these went on to Ceylon and then back through Indonesia and southeast Asia. Some went from China to Vietnam. Others from China went to Korea or Japan. Chinese Buddhists were the most extensive of Buddhist travellers.

Indonesian monks went to Nalanda in India to study, also as missionaries to southeast Asia. Monks at Srivijaya (Sumatra) taught Sanskrit to Chinese monks and to others who came there for higher studies of Buddhism. The Japanese went to China as the holy land of Buddhism where they visited the famous monasteries and temples. Korean monks helped to establish Buddhism in Japan.

There was a most significant cultural contact of Ceylon with Burma, Thailand, Cambodia, and Laos, especially in the period after the twelfth century when Ceylon was spreading Theravada Buddhism throughout this region, sending monks to these countries and receiving monks for training and ordination.

The multicultural community thus established was founded on belief in Buddha and in the doctrine that he communicated to mankind. Buddha himself was the primary interest, the primary allegiance, the subject of thought, conversation, and teaching within this community. To his followers Buddha was a special manifestation of the final truth of things. In his teachings men throughout this region found a saving wisdom and a spiritual discipline that enabled them to deal effectively with the human condition and finally to obtain release from the conditioned world into the realm of the unconditioned. No other personality in this region of Asia is in any way comparable to Buddha. He remains a unique phenomenon in the history of these peoples. Within this region Buddha is not only the Asian personality par excellence, he is the only personality known throughout Asia. The historical experience of Buddha is the only personal experience communicated to so many Asian peoples.

The spiritual heritage shared in common by Buddha's followers was founded in the common experience of the human condition as impermanent, sorrowful, and insubstantial. Awareness that life is a painful experience was not confined to Buddhists, yet it was Buddha who first thoroughly examined this experience of pain, investigated its causes with such insight, and proposed a remedy of such absolute proportions and with such immediate and universal appeal. There was not the slightest doubt in the Buddhist community of Asia that the way had been found, the victory had been achieved, the basic mystery of life had been solved. That is what gave to the community such strength. The effective healing of sorrow now depended only on following the Buddha Path in company with vast numbers of other Asian peoples who belonged to the same spiritual community.

Buddhism also brought to this region a common piety and a common meditative discipline. This might be called the art of inwardness. Piety and meditation: these seem to be opposites; in reality they are similar. Recollection in piety is for the simple folk of Asia what mental concentration is to the more learned and more practised. This meditative discipline, an adaptation and complete transformation of the ancient Indian Yoga, was communicated to the other countries of Asia so extensively that the one basic discipline is practised in China, Japan, and Tibet, in Thailand, Burma, and Ceylon. The piety too, the intense devotion to Buddha, is a common feature throughout this area, despite all the differences that have arisen due to the diversity of historical and cultural circumstances.

Another doctrine that became common to this entire region during the Buddhist period was the doctrine of karma, the doctrine that there is an absolute moral determinism in life. The sorrow men experience in life has been determined by their own needs either in this life or in a previous life. This doctrine, held in common by the Hindu and the Buddhist worlds, became the common possession of this region. The significance of this doctrine in the life of Asian peoples is very great. It altered the entire moral context of life.

Also communicated at this time was a common spiritual institution, the Buddhist monastery. This was the essential instrument of Buddhist life. A great number of monasteries were set up in every country of this region. While each monastic establishment remained independent of the others, there was a common tradition represented by all. All lived according to the same basic regulations. The monastery was the centre for intensive personal development for those willing to become followers of Buddha in the highest sense. The monasteries were also centres for the development and study of Buddhist thought traditions and for the origin of Buddhist missionary efforts. A follower of Buddha would feel at home and in familiar surroundings in any one of these monasteries.

Buddhist monks constituted a new social class that acquired status throughout this region. The ideal of voluntary poverty was established as an honourable ideal, admired and often longed for by those burdened with the complexities of secular life and the responsibilities of public office. This status was more admired at some times and places than at others. In China the status of the monks declined considerably in favour of the Confucian ideal of the gentleman. But even there a vestige of deep admiration remained for this class of persons. In Japan until the sixteenth century monks such as Muso often held high advisory positions in the government of the country. In Japan and in much of southeast Asia the monks carried the tradition of learning in the society for centuries. Even to this day education in many areas of southeast Asia is carried on primarily by Buddhist monks.

Buddhism also gave to this region a sacred literature. This was spread across these many countries and translated into some twenty languages. Hindu literature, especially the Ramayana, was widespread throughout southeast Asia. Confucian literature was communicated to the countries surrounding China. But in its volume and universality there was nothing comparable to the Buddhist literature communicated to this region.

The corpus of Buddhist literature is one, even though there does exist a significant division between the Hinayana and the Mahayana literature. Not all of this literature is found throughout this region, but only in the greater centres, in India, China, and Japan. Yet if very few works are well known throughout the entire area, there is a sharing of a common literature, and large portions of this literature are found in every part of the Buddhist world. The essential elements of the entire tradition are found in each of its parts. The Mahayana literature is less widespread than the Hina-

yana, since the Mahayana had only limited contact with
Ceylon, Burma, Thailand, Cambodia, Laos. The northern
regions from Tibet to Japan possessed the major elements
of the Hinayana scriptures in the Sarvastivada school along
with the scriptures of the Mahayana tradition. The Hinayana
was an essential part of the Mahayana tradition. The Mahayana was not an essential part of the Hinayana tradition.

Common to this region also is an entire complex of ideas
and attitudes of the intellectual order. The most significant
of these ideas is that of sunyata, of emptiness, the central
idea of the Mahayana tradition, which is only a continuation
and development of the anatta teaching of the Hinayana.
This concept, spread throughout Asia, expresses best what
has traditionally been considered in the West as the "Oriental" attitude to reality. "Sunyata" is to a large part of the
Oriental world what "being" is to the Occident.

There are also the basic ideas contained in the *Abhidharma*
literature of the Hinayana schools. This extensive classification of the physical, psychological, emotional, and moral
phenomena has given a common set of terms to the entire
Buddhist world. These constitute the distinctive range of discourse that is proper to Buddhists everywhere.

Scholars in the learned centres, popular preachers in the
smallest villages, have read the same scriptural traditions,
have commented on the same basic doctrines. They have
centred the mind on the same Buddha personality, have
quoted the same phrases, have worked out the same basic
pattern of release from the impermanent, sorrowful, insubstantial world. Thus a common world of thought has been
established. The Chinese pilgrims who travelled this entire
region found everywhere a home, a common literature, a
world of converse with which all Buddhists were familiar.

Common emotional attitudes and responses were also
communicated through Buddhism. This is not to say that

the emotional lives of the Chinese and Japanese Buddhists are the same, or that the Singhalese and the Burmese are the same. Indeed they are vastly different. Yet there is also present an emotional identity that can be recognized. This can be seen particularly in the Buddhist monks who derive from different ethnic backgrounds but who are profoundly conditioned in their emotional life through the common values, the common discipline of their life situation, the common intellectual development, the common path of release.

The primary element in this emotional response of the Buddhist community of Asia is based on the attitude that this world is the realm of unreality, that emotional attachment to this world brings only sorrow, that a decisive emotional disengagement must take place if a person is to be released from this life-sorrow. Once the follower of Buddha has understood these truths in some depth and has followed the Eightfold Path to liberation there descends upon him a remarkable calm in the midst of the daily life anxieties that are common to all mankind. The release attained is reflected in what might be called the inner serenity that is the most characteristic emotional quality of Buddhism in its vital periods.

Another characteristic of Buddhist emotional life is an attitude of sympathy towards all living beings, a deep aversion to killing in any form, a sympathy for those who suffer, although this sympathy, this feeling of identity with the sufferings of others, is intended to be without personal emotional involvement.

The greatest emotional changes affected by Buddhism were those brought about among the Mongol, Tibetan, and Thai peoples. These were all peoples with aggressive and warring instincts until they were profoundly changed in their emotional life by conversion to Buddhism. They lost much of their aggressiveness and settled into a generally peaceful life. Among both the Mongols and the Tibetans an extraordinary proportion of the men became Buddhist monks. At one time almost half the Mongols became monks. In Tibet there have been times when a third of the men were monks. This emotional change was strengthened by the entry of these peoples into a higher civilization status through their conversion to Buddhism. They attained a more spiritual vision of life and a higher intellectual development than anything they had previously known.

Another achievement of the Buddhist community in Asia was the establishment of common elements in the art of Asia. This can be clearly seen in architecture. Here as elsewhere diversity exists along with identity. The stupas, dagobas, and pagodas of Asia are all different in different regions, yet they are all variations of a single structure, the burial mound for the relics of Buddha. Originally the stupa was also a cosmic symbol to assist in integrating man and the human world into the cosmic order. Yet even more important, the stupa, the dagoba, the pagoda established for the believer the Buddha presence. In its very structure it recalls the earthly presence of Buddha. The reminder that he also has passed away recalls the impermanence of all things. The whole structure indicates the way of salvation from the confinement of the human condition.

Besides the stupas and pagodas there are the monasteries, temples, and shrines that are found in vast numbers throughout the Buddhist region of Asia. These structures are the most frequently seen structures on the landscape. In southeast Asia particularly the building of pagodas and temples has gone to extravagant lengths. This is true in Burma particularly, where pagodas are established everywhere. So in the great centres of Thailand, Cambodia, Laos, and Vietnam, we find everywhere the architectural evidence of Buddha's presence.

Nowhere in these regions of Asia is one very far from a Buddhist structure of some kind. In India the Buddhist establishments were destroyed more completely than in any other country of Asia. Yet there once existed in almost every sizable settlement of east and southeast Asia a Buddhist structure of some kind, which can still be seen in Japan and above all in southeast Asia. In China the structures of the great Buddhist periods of China's history have fallen into ruins or have been destroyed by the many wars and uprisings that have taken place. But even so the number of Buddhist structures is large in some areas of China. In east and southeast Asia generally the traveller is constantly aware of the Buddhist horizon that surrounds him. Buddhist structures have been the sights most longed for by the traveller at the end of the day. There he would find shelter, refreshment, protection, companionship. But above all he finds in his travels that the most basic transformation that man has given to nature in this region is found in its Buddhist architecture. Everywhere there is evidence that the traveller is passing through a sacred Buddhaland.

The effect of Buddhism in Asian art can be clearly seen in the sculpture of the region. There is an extensive Hindu tradition of sculpture in India and in some parts of southeast Asia, particularly at Angkor prior to the thirteenth century. But outside of this tradition it might be said that the sculpture, especially the figure sculpture, of this entire region is Buddhist both in subject matter and in feeling. This is true particularly of the sculpture of China. By far the greater part of Chinese sculpture is of Buddhist themes in such centres as Yun-kang, Lungmen and Tienlung Shan. There are other sculpture works in Asia, but these do not amount to anything like the impressiveness in volume, universality, or variety that is found in Buddhist sculpture. Within the one tradition there is, of course, great difference between Chinese and Japanese Buddhist sculpture. Both these differ from the Buddhist sculpture of India. All these in turn differ from the sculpture of Angkor and Borobudur. The Buddha and Boddisattva figures of the Mahayana lands have a depth of compassion that is not present in the Buddha figures of the Hinayana lands of Buddhism, which have an isolation and

an inwardness that differ markedly from the heavenly providence manifested in many of the Mahayana works of the
north. Nor is there any of the tenderness manifested in the
smiling Bodhisattva figures of the Wei period of China. Yet
there is a profound continuity that extends from the Buddha
figures of Mathura and Sarnath to the Buddha figures of
Yun-kang, Lungmen and Nara, and also to the Buddha
figures of southeast Asia. The common element in Buddhist
sculpture can be seen particularly in the portrayal of the unconditioned world beyond the world of time and change. All
Buddhist figures reflect this. There is in them an intersection
of the planes of reality, the phenomenal and the transphenomenal within a specifically Buddhist context. In this
portrayal of inwardness, in the calm experience of the unconditioned realm completely beyond yet totally within the
world of time, Buddhist sculpture makes its greatest impress
and achieves its own greatest identity and universality. We
can observe also in Buddhist sculpture an iconographical
repertory that is common to the entire region. There are
the facial features, the halo, the bodily postures, the mudra
or hand-signs, the type of clothing, and the lotus symbol.
There is seldom any difficulty in identifying Buddhist sculpture wherever it is found in Asia.

CHAPTER XVIII

BUDDHISM AND THE WEST

Until recently, Western knowledge of Buddhism existed within three groups: A limited group of scholars with access to the original documents of Buddhism; a group of serious thinkers in the realm of religion and philosophy whose knowledge is mainly derived from secondary sources; a group of persons dissatisfied with Western spiritual traditions who have sought some strange, esoteric, spiritual experience by contact with Buddhism. These last have frequently shown an excess of enthusiasm, a lack of soundness in their understanding of Buddhism, and a slighting attitude towards other spiritual traditions. A scholarly study of Buddhism reveals that the main esoteric elements of Buddhism arose a thousand years after Buddhism came into existence. While these esoteric, Tantric, elements of Buddhism are extremely important in studying the entire Buddhist tradition, they are not essential to a thorough study of the main developments of Hinayana and Mahayana which constitute the real significance of Buddhism in the wider humanist culture of mankind. One of the great values of contemporary scholarship is that it has done way with theosophist distortions in our understanding of Buddhism and has given us a clear picture of the historical setting in which Buddhism arose, the early teachings, the manner in which these developed, the schools of thought that emerged, the art and literature that has been produced under Buddhist inspiration.

Now two other groups of persons acquainted with Buddhism are emerging in our society. One is composed of students who have read extensively in Buddhist writings during their college years under the guidance of teachers with a scholarly acquaintance with the material. The other is composed of persons of general intellectual ability and interest who read the excellent anthologies of Buddhist writings available in paperback editions. Both of these groups tend to have a good understanding of Buddhism as a tradition that has important things to say to all mankind.

It is clear that Buddhism ranks with Hinduism, Confucianism, and Islam among the four most significant spiritual forces of the non-Christian world that have affected the destinies of mankind. To be ignorant of Buddhism is to be ignorant of a large part of man's spiritual, intellectual, and cultural formation. This spirituality and this culture are no more difficult than any of the other major traditions of mankind. All the basic spiritual traditions of man are open, clear, direct expressions of the manner in which man has structured his personal and social life in order to give it some higher, transcendent significance. These spiritual disciplines have enabled man to deal with the problem of suffering and eventually to attain some kind of liberation from the afflictions that mark his temporal existence. What Buddhism has done belongs among the highest moral, spiritual, intellectual, and cultural achievements ever attained by man.

In the future there can be no adequate humanistic study of man that does not give considerable consideration to Buddhism. In previous centuries there was a lack of awareness of Buddhism that excused the West from including in its study the accomplishments of this tradition. But that period is gone. The evidence is available, the communication is in process. It only needs to be properly received and appreciated. Not to do this is to leave our humanism in a retarded state of development.

There are two great spiritual endeavours that characterize the present age. One is the effort to interpret the new scientific technological age in the light of man's traditional spiritual disciplines. The other is the effort of traditional spiritual disciplines to enter into communion with each other. This last effort at establishing a world context for man's spiritual and intellectual development has just begun. From the Christian side the Second Vatican Council took a great step forward when it established a special secretariat for communication with the other religious and spiritual traditions of mankind. This is in modern times a task similar to the task of the early Fathers of the Church in establishing of a deep communication with the thought, culture, and spirituality of the Hellenic world. A new patristic age is in process of formation, an age vaster in its scope than the earlier patristic age. We can expect it to be equally more fruitful in its consequences, for it is leading towards a new world culture in which all the world traditions will have their finest and fullest expression.

WORKS REFERRED TO
IN THE TEXT

Anguttara Nikaya, Eng. tr., *The Book of Gradual Sayings,* 5 vols., by F. L. Woodward and E. M. Hare, London, Pali Text Society, 1932–1955.

Astasahasrika Prajnaparamita Sutra, Eng. tr., *Selected Sayings from the Perfection of Perfect Wisdom,* by Edward Conze, London, The Buddhist Society, 1955.

Bodhicaryavatara, Santi Deva, selected and translated as *The Path of Light,* 2nd ed., by L. D. Barnett, London, John Murray, 1947.

Buddhacarita, Ashvaghosa, Eng. tr. in *Buddhist Mahayana Texts,* SBE, vol. 49, by E. B. Cowell, Oxford University Press, 1894.

Diamond Sutra, SBE, vol. 49, Eng. tr., by M. F. Max Muller, Oxford University Press, 1894.

Digha Nikaya, Eng. tr., *Dialogues of the Buddha,* 3 vols. SBB (reprint), by T. W. and C. A. F. Rhys Davids, London, Luzac, 1956–1959.

Fa-hsien, *A Record of Buddhistic Kingdoms,* Eng. tr., by James Legge, Oxford, Clarendon Press, 1886.

Hsüan-tsang, *Buddhist Records of the Western World,* 4 vols. (reprint), Eng. tr., by Samuel Beal, Calcutta, Susil Gupta, 1957.

Itivuttakam, Eng. tr., *The Minor Anthologies,* by F. L. Woodward, SBB, London, Luzac, 1948.

Kathavatthu, Eng. tr., *Points of Controversy,* by Shwe An Aung and Mrs. G. Rhys Davids, PTS, London, Luzac, 1915.

Khuddakapatha, Eng. tr., *The Minor Readings and Illustrator,* by Bhikkhu Nanamoli, PTS, London, Luzac, 1960.

186 WORKS REFERRED TO IN THE TEXT

Lankavatarasutra, Eng. tr., by Daisetz Suzuki, London, Routledge and Kegan Paul, 1932.

Lotus Sutra, Eng. tr., by H. Kern, SBE, xxi, Oxford, 1909.

Madhyamakakarika by Nagarjuna, German tr., *Die Mittlere Lehre des Nagarjuna,* by M. Walleser, Heidelberg, 1912.

Mahavastu, 3 vols., Eng. tr., by J. J. Hones, SBB, London, Luzac, 1949–1956.

Mahayanasamgrahah, French tr., *La Somme du Grand Véhicule d'Asanga,* Louvain, 1938.

Majjhima Nikaya, Eng. tr., *The Middle Length Discourses,* 3 vols., by I. B. Horner, PTS, London, Luzac, 1954–1959.

Milindapanho, Eng. tr., *The Questions of King Milinda,* 2 vols., by T. W. Rhys Davids, SBE, Oxford, 1894.

Samdhinirmocana Sutra, Tibetan version ed. and tr. into French by Étienne Lamotte, Paris, Adrien Maisonneuve, 1935.

Smaller Sukhivativyuha Sutra, Eng. tr. in *Buddhist Mahayana Texts,* vol. 49, by F. Max Muller, SBE, Oxford, Clarendon, 1894.

Sukhivativyuha Sutra, Eng. tr. *Land of Bliss Sutra,* in *Buddhist Mahayana Texts,* vol. 49, by F. Max Muller, SBE, Oxford, Clarendon, 1894.

Sutta Nipata, Eng. tr. *Buddha's Teachings,* in HOS Vol. 37, by Lord Chalmers, Cambridge, Mass., Harvard University Press, 1932.

Sutta Nipata, Eng. tr., *Woven Cadences of Early Buddhists,* by E. M. Hare, London, Oxford University Press, 1945.

Suzuki, Daisetz, *Essays in Zen Buddhism,* 3rd series (reprint), London, Rider, 1958.

Svetesvatara Upanishad, Eng. tr., by F. Max Muller, SBE, New York, 1897.

Suvarnaprabhasottama-Sutra, German tr., *Das Goldglanz-sutra,* from Chinese version of I-tsing, by J. Nobel, Leiden, E. J. Brill, 1938.

Udana, Eng. tr. in *The Minor Anthologies,* by F. L. Woodward, London, 1935.

Vasubandhu, *Vijnaptimatratasiddhi; Vimsatika,* Eng. tr., *Treatise in Twenty Stanzas on Representation Only,* from Chinese version of Hsüan-tsang, by Clarence H. Hamilton, New Haven, American Oriental Society, 1938.

Vimalikirtinirdesa, French tr., *L'Enseignement de Vimalakirti,* by Étienne Lamotte, Louvain, 1962.

Visuddhimagga by Buddhaghosa, Eng. tr., *The Path of Purification,* 2nd ed., by Bhikkhu Nyanamoli, Colombo, Gunasena, 1964.

SELECT BIBLIOGRAPHY

Ch'en, Kenneth K. S., *Buddhism in China,* Princeton, N.J., Princeton University Press, 1964.

Conze, Edward, *Buddhist Texts through the Ages,* New York, Philosophical Library, 1954.

—————— *Buddhist Thought in India,* London, Allen & Unwin, 1962.

Dumoulin, Heinrich, *A History of Zen Buddhism,* tr. from German, New York, Pantheon, 1963.

Dutt, Sukumar, *Buddhist Monks and Monasteries of India,* London, Allen & Unwin, 1962.

Lamotte, Étienne, *Histoire du Bouddhisme Indien des Origines à l'Ère Saka,* Louvain, Publications Universitaires, 1958.

Pande, Govind C., *The Origins of Buddhism.* University of Allahabad, 1957.

Pratt, J. B., *The Pilgrimage of Buddhism,* New York, Macmillan, 1928.

Saunders, E. Dale, *Buddhism in Japan,* University of Pennsylvania Press, 1964.

Soothill, W. E., *The Lotus of the Wonderful Law,* Oxford, Clarendon Press, 1930.

Thomas, E. J. *The Life of Buddha as Legend and History,* London, Lund Humphries, 1927.

—————— *The History of Buddhist Thought,* 2nd ed., New York, Barnes and Noble, 1951.

Wright, Arthur E., *Buddhism in Chinese History* (reprint), New York, Atheneum, 1965.